I0790408

Edited by Norma Hashim and translated by Yousef M. Aljamal, the forthcoming volume, published by Malaysia's Saba Islamic Media, includes a range of young detainees. Some contributors, like Malaak al-Khatib, a 14-year-old girl captured while walking home from school at the end of 2014, are familiar, having won brief fame during their detentions. Many are not, although their experiences – violence, torture, isolation – inevitably are.

Most valuably, *Dreaming of Freedom* encourages its participants to speak naturally in their own voices, rather than seeking to depoliticize them or impose false notions of "innocence" on those who have participated in a just anti-colonial struggle. While Israeli soldiers captured Malaak as she picked flowers, others, like Ammar Adeli, unapologetically threw stones – and, in his case, were detained their first time.

"I insisted on participating in our Palestinian struggle," the 14-year-old says. *"It was not just a game to me, but rather a cause, much older than I was."*

By placing Israel's military detention of Palestinian children in its full context – not only the Israeli occupation itself, but also Palestinian resistance to it – *Dreaming of Freedom* offers valuable insight into the lives of children whose forays against heavily-armed soldiers, walls and tanks have inspired millions. And by refusing to reduce them to mere objects of humanitarian concern, instead leaving their motivations intact for readers to consider, it portrays them authentically, as standard-bearers of a cause and political actors in their own right. 🙶

~ Samidoun Palestinian Prisoner Solidarity Network

❝ Childhood is a time for joy, growth and love. But not for the children of Palestine, who know only fear, anger and oppression. Like a piece of broken glass, they have suffered and continue to suffer from the mental and psychological torment that deprives them of a normal childhood. The footnotes after each story says it all – none of the children featured in this book went on to develop into a balanced, healthy adult, and perhaps never will. The stories contained within this book capture one of the most overlooked aspects of the cruel war on Palestine – the children, who represent the future of this broken nation. Although many of the children displayed resilience and defiance despite torture and imprisonment (some repeated times), we ask ourselves, are these normal emotional and psychological processes for children? The answer is obvious. A childhood lost can never be regained. It is time to stop the oppression, and allow the people, particularly the children, a chance to heal. **❞**

~ Dr Musa Mohd Nordin
Chairman, Viva Palestina Malaysia

❝ The stories of these Palestinian kids plead to us like angels. These kids are the future. If we don't do enough to save and protect them from Israel, we are doomed. This book shows us how to act responsibly. **❞**

~ Refaat Alareer
Editor, *Gaza Writes Back*

Dreaming of Freedom
Palestinian Child Prisoners Speak

شيلوك هم بلادك في اللفة من انت صغير

"They made you bear the burden of your homeland while you were still a baby wrapped in blankets."

Shayalouk/Mays Shalash

In memory of child prisoner Ayman Abbasi,
who was interviewed for this book,
but did not live to see it published.

Dreaming of Freedom
Palestinian Child Prisoners Speak

Edited by Norma Hashim
Translated by Yousef M. Aljamal
Foreword by Richard Falk

Piedmont Press is an imprint of Just World Books, LLC

Edited by: Norma Hashim
All contributions (text and image) used with the permission of the owners

Translated by: Yousef M. Aljamal
Design by: Red Bamboo Creative Sdn Bhd
Cover illustration by: Mahmoud Salameh
Typesetting by: Lapiz

Mohammad Saba'aneh is a Palestinian cartoonist from Jenin who spent 5 months in an Israeli prison in 2013.

Contents

Foreword

Richard Falk

WHAT strikes me most directly after reading these moving statements by Palestinian child prisoners is the aura of state terror that pervades the lives of all Palestinians living under occupation. Horrifying as is the experience of these children, mainly mid-teenagers, the deeper horror is the degree to which the entire community of Palestinians is scarred for life by Israeli brutality. Of course, it is the stone throwing children that bear the brunt of the violence that is reported by the vivid statements compiled here, but their younger siblings and older parents and relatives are also being scarred for life by the arrest and interrogation process developed by Israel that seems calculated to be as intimidating as possible.

Reading through such pages of torment, a pattern of abuse clearly emerges that exhibits Israel's total disregard for international human rights and international humanitarian law as it applies to these young Palestinians, who are totally vulnerable to such oppressive tactics. Although international humanitarian law fails to focus with sufficient specificity on the vulnerability of children, there are some general measures of protection given in Articles 71-74 of the Fourth Geneva Convention, which ensures that any civilian subject to occupation who is charged with criminal activity shall be informed in writing in a language that he or she understands, is assured the right to the assistance of a lawyer, and must be given the opportunity to present evidence in defense. It is no surprise, based on our knowledge of Israel's apartheid administration of Palestinians living under occupation that none of these rights are recognized and respected. Indeed, the daily reality of life for Palestinians of all ages is one of rightlessness and unconditional vulnerability.

Despite the generality of abuse to which Palestinians of all ages are subjected to throughout their entire life, it is important to take account of the particular forms of experience that are the tragic destiny of Palestinian children, realities that begin from the earliest stages of childhood. What these reports convey as a result of their overlapping accounts narrated with a concreteness that makes the reader confident about the credibility of the stories being told. This credibility is further reinforced by the consistent reports of respected Palestinian and Israeli NGOs concerned with the protection of human rights of those being subjected to the rigors of Israeli criminal law enforcement. In other words, from everything we know, there is every reason to place trust in the accuracy of these first-person accounts, and given the careful method by which this material was assembled it is possible to construct an accurate portrayal of this pattern of lawless law.

Among the features of this pattern that particularly stand out, I would mention the practice of apprehending Palestinian youth accused of resistance activity in the middle of the night in the presence of the entire family including very young siblings. The accused youth is literally seized from his home and family without being informed of what he is alleged to have done, with parents being given no idea where he is being taken and for how long. Invariably, as well, the child being taken captive is painfully tied and blindfolded often in the presence of his family, thrown onto the floor of a military car, and generally badly beaten while being taken to an interrogation center or some preliminary holding area. The interrogation process is itself completely alienating and calculated to overcome even the most stubborn refusal of a teenage boy to cooperate with his jailors by acknowledging guilt.

It seems clear that the 'crime' that almost all of these Palestinian children are accused is throwing stones at vehicles that belong to Israeli security forces or settlers. There is no claim by the Israeli authorities that these stones caused any injury or even damage, but the allegations are treated as if involving the most serious imaginable crimes. As has been observed by progressive Israeli journalists and others, the throwing of stones should be principally understood as forms of symbolic violence expressive of the inherent right to resist unlawful and abusive occupation. What is more, such stone throwing is consistently met with excessive force by Israel that constitutes violence of a much more punitive and consequential nature, and seems inflicted with an intent to intimidate not only the immediate victim but Palestinian youth in general.

In the end, the tactics used by Israel are mostly successful in extracting confessions from the Palestinian children, seemingly regardless of whether the allegations are accurate or mistaken. What we take away from the 'confessions' reported in these statements is an utter inability to determine whether it is accurate or fake. As the prisoners are being threatened with continuous beatings, contrived reports that others have independently confirmed the accusations, prison 'plants' or 'snitches' who mislead the accused on behalf of the captors, and a variety of abusive practices, it is hardly surprising that the will of these children is eventually broken in almost all cases. In a manner that I encountered in apartheid South Africa maintaining innocence is usually punished worse than confessions, whether true of false, and thus there is no incentive whatsoever to hold out. What is even more dehumanizing, is the demand of Israeli officials that these Palestinian teenagers implicate their friends and neighbors. It is evident that several of the narrations compiled here report great courage in holding out by refusing to confess, although in such a confined setting where the difference between guilt and innocence is obliterated the significance of such a sacrificial resolve of steadfastness is rarely appreciated or even known in the outside world.

Another striking feature of this arrest and interrogation experience is the punitive reliance by Israel on post-release punishment in the form of house arrest. Several of these young Palestinians declare that they would prefer confinement in an Israel prison than enduring house arrest. At first, this preference is difficult to comprehend. On reflection, it becomes more understandable given the nature of life under occupation that allows so few opportunities for satisfaction, and house arrest is a tantalizing deprivation of the camaraderie of friendship and neighborhood life.

These Palestinian children express a shared feeling of humiliation that seems to be even more painful for them than the beatings received. The word (izlaal in Arabic) recurs repeatedly in these narratives, and I think testifies to the dehumanizing effects caused by feelings of helplessness and futility, which Israel seeks to induce so as to give rise to an atmosphere among Palestinians of resignation, if not spiritual surrender. A similar approach is evident in relation to house demolitions that are justified in the name of security, but are carried out for the sake of collective punishment and intimidation. Jeff Halper, a respected Israeli critic of the practice estimates that less than 1% of all house demolitions have a genuine security justification.

There are several conclusions that emerge from this deeply moving collection of separate but interconnected witnessing by these Palestinian children. First of all, the urgent need for a distinct international treaty devoted to the situation of children living under conditions of prolonged occupation. Realizing that Israeli occupation has lasted almost half a century with no end in sight, it is intolerable from the perspective of human dignity and human rights, to fail to offer much more concrete protection, including procedures for redress of grievances. Secondly, we need studies of the longer term effects in terms of trauma of such arrest and interrogation experiences, as well as on the impact on families and communities not only of the dynamics of victimization, but also of the shared sense of hopelessness that is the inevitable by-product of witnessing a brother or son dragged away by abusive soldiers in the middle of the night. And thirdly, we need widespread dissemination of these Israeli policies and practices, especially as carried out with the evident intent of immobilizing resistance to an unlawful occupation that has gone on far too long.

In this spirit, I commend a close reading of *Dreaming of Freedom: Palestinian Child Prisoners Speak*. With such knowledge, solidarity with the Palestinian struggle for freedom and dignity becomes almost a psychological inevitability and an even more urgent moral imperative of our world than we previously realized.

3 May 2016

Professor Falk is Albert G. Milbank Professor of International Law and Practice, Emeritus at Princeton University, and was Distinguished Visiting Professor in Global & International Studies, University of California at Santa Barbara. He completed a six year term as UN Special Rapporteur on Human Rights in Occupied Palestine in 2014.

Introduction

Wasfi Izzat Kabaha

ALL Palestinians, regardless of age, are liable to Israeli arrests, without any regard to International Law. As part of a systematic policy, the Israeli Occupation has targeted Palestinian children, subjecting them to murder, injury, arrest, detention and trial.

The issue of child prisoners in Israeli Occupation jails is particularly sensitive, as it reveals their suffering (and that of their families) in contrast to the protection that they are entitled under Article 77 of the *Additional Protocol 1 (1977) to the Geneva Convention (1949)*.

Arresting Palestinian minors is one of the clearest pieces of evidence of the arbitrary practices by Israel and its lack of commitment to International Law, which provides protection for Palestinian children. Palestinian children represent the face of the Palestinian suffering caused by the Israeli Occupation and the Israeli Prison Service, which sees in Palestinian children their enemies and a threat to their Zionist project. They treat them as potential resistance fighters who will bear the seeds of resistance and rebellion against the Israeli Occupation. They aim to harm them, as they see in these children the power of revenge against those who killed their parents, committed massacres against their families and confiscated their ancestors' lands.

The Israeli Occupation targets the children of Jerusalem – one of the most important cities in the struggle against the Israeli Occupation – even more than their counterparts in other cities and towns. They aim to brainwash these children to change their values and beliefs and win the battle over Jerusalem, by producing Palestinians who care little for their cause. This campaign is exemplified by the case of Ahmad Manasarh, who was barely 13 years old when arrested in October 2015 and convicted by an Israeli court in March 2016 of two counts of attempted murder. The photos of Ahmad bleeding on the ground while Israeli settlers were assaulting him, as well as the stories of his interrogation 'went viral' across social media. He is currently detained in a 'Reform Centre' in the village of Yarka in Occupied Galilee.

The Israeli Occupation cannot provide a suitable protection environment for Palestinian children as it is the source of their ongoing suffering. Amidst a continuing deafening international silence, it places them in miserable living conditions, behind bars. International intervention is needed and we all have a responsibility to pressure the Israeli Occupation to abide by International Law and cease its violations of Palestinian children, who just like other children, deserve to grow up in peace. This is the only way to achieve a real and lasting peace in Palestine – otherwise, tears will continue to be shed, and wounds bleed.

Whilst Palestinian children have experienced all forms of sorrow since the Nakba of 1948, they also were at the forefront of one of the most important uprisings in history, the first

Palestinian uprising in 1987, which came to be known as the 'Uprising of Stones'. These children had grown up in refugee camps and had always had food insecurity. They tasted the bitterness of losing loved ones as a result of the continuing Occupation and its targeting of their homes. These children lived through curfews that denied them formal education as they were prevented from attending school. They saw their houses demolished and bullets from Occupation soldiers take the best of their friends. These children still hold to what remains of their childhood despite the sorrow and pain, and they are still dreaming of enjoying their childhood just like other children in the world.

The impact of arrest on children is greater than that of adults, because of their lack of experience and the lack of defense mechanisms to these situations. Consequently, children who have been imprisoned are extremely likely to suffer from a range of severe psychological problems, including anxiety and face enormous adaptation problems upon release, with their families and friends.

The testimonies that Norma Hashim has documented in this book reveal the suffering of Palestinian children such as former child prisoner Mussallam Odeh from Jerusalem who was arrested 15 times, although just 13 years old. Norma Hashim's efforts are extremely important, as it gives the world an idea about how Palestinian children are suffering under the Israeli Occupation, by presenting the stories of 24 child prisoners, in addition to the five stories of the Hares boys.

In the ongoing Al-Quds Intifada, Palestinian children have played a major role – in the first few months of it many of them threw stones at the Israeli Occupation soldiers. The Israeli military has tried to destroy the morale of children, families and neighbours, by storming the children's homes at night and making it very difficult for their families. They have turned countless homes upside down and arrested these children in order to stop the momentum of the Intifada.

Targeting Palestinian children in the manner described throughout this book violates Article 16 of the *Convention on the Rights of the Child (1989)*, which states that:

"1. No child shall be subjected to arbitrary or unlawful interference with his or her privacy, family, or correspondence, nor to unlawful attacks on his or her honour and reputation.

2. The child has the right to the protection of the law against such interference or attacks."

The Israeli legal system is a tool in the hands of the military. As clearly articulated throughout this book by the affected children, Israeli courts are routinely involved in the harassment of Palestinian child prisoners. Some of the children in this book have been placed under house arrest and some even deported to other cities, as has happened with Ahmad Ghaith, aged 11, who since this book was researched has been deported from Jerusalem for two months and ordered to pay a 4,000 NIS fine.

Despite all of these concerted attacks, Palestinian children grow more resilient to the Israeli Occupation. Their stories reflect their manhood, courage and strength while facing Israeli interrogators and jailers, who deny them their innocence and cause them to mature, prematurely.

The stories in this book could inform legal actions against individuals and organisations acting on behalf of the Israeli Occupation for crimes against the Palestinian children. It brilliantly documents the various stages of arrest and it proves the extent of the torture that the children have experienced, as well as the deprivation of their family life and education.

This book is an important document that proves the barbarity of the Israeli Occupation and exposes it to the whole world. The Israeli entity acts above the law and is anti-democratic. I hope that one day the testimonies in this book will assist in cases against individuals before the International Criminal Court in The Hague, as we seek justice for all Palestinian children.

10 May 2016

Wasfi Izzat Kabaha is a former detainee & former Palestinian Minister of Prisoners' Affairs.

The following interviews were conducted by
Fayhaa Shalash in 2015.

A Child of Shuhada Street

Yazan Al-Shrbati
Age 14
Hebron

I DON'T expect any child's life in the rest of the world to be like mine and those who live on my street. Our daily life has turned into a battle to exist with dignity, although we, as children, know little about battles – we mostly think about playing and having fun.

Shuhada Street (which means Martyrs' Street) to the south of Hebron is a narrow street, which with the number of soldiers, settlers, checkpoints and fences feels narrower than you could possibly imagine. Yet this street is a part of me, as much as I am a part of it. I couldn't leave it behind even if I wanted to.

Yazan being detained by Israeli police on the way home from school.

Since the start of this Occupation, the people living on Shuhada Street have become targets for settlers who are doing their best to take over our homes while being paid to do so. We have known this since we were breastfed by our mothers! Simply because we are not normal Palestinians, we are the people of Shuhada Street.

One Saturday I was walking in the street trying to live just another day. I was feeling more comfortable than usual, because it was the Jewish Shabbat which normally meant the settlers would not trouble us and I could walk slowly. I heard some noises but I didn't pay attention to them. I continued walking but was suddenly stopped by a number of Israeli settlers.

I thought they would, as usual, only curse me then I could continue walking. But this time after one of them cursed me, another one spat at me. I stopped in my tracks. The third settler began attacking me. They all then started beating me together. I no longer stayed silent and started screaming at them loudly.

A soldier came and pushed them away, but then grabbed my shoulder, playing the usual role in the play that we have all got used to. I thought he had some humanity, but I was wrong. He kicked my body and hit me in the head as I screamed in pain and pleaded for any Palestinians around to help. I listened to the settlers fabricating a story, telling the soldiers that it was me who had assaulted them first. I was in disbelief.

The soldier took me to a nearby military post. Police officers came and took me to a police station at the Kiryaat Arbaa colony. I was taken to the interrogation room, not knowing why, as I was the victim of an assault. The interrogator tried to make me say something. I refused, insisting on my innocence. I was still trying to work out exactly how bad my wounds were after the beatings of the settlers and the police.

I spent a whole day at the police station. One of the officers brought a piece of paper in Hebrew and forced me to sign it without knowing anything about its contents. I found out later that it said: *"I will not create any problems in the future."* I was photographed and then released on bail. I was not arrested for a long time, but that experience changed me in many different ways.

Imprisonment is not the most serious offense committed against the Palestinian children of Shuhada Street. Every minute under Occupation at the mercy of the settlers in this Martyrs' Street we are subjected to thousands of violations including police dogs and settlers throwing stones and Molotov cocktails at us. They scream at us and beat us. All of this disturbs the tranquility of our lives from the day we come into this world. Arresting me without committing any crime gave me more determination to continue to exist here.

I still live in my family's house in my street, in my little neighborhood. I will never leave. ♦

** Yazan still goes to school but living on Shuhada Street in Hebron, a place separated by the Occupation from other parts of the city, means he has to cross multiple checkpoints when he goes to school in the morning, and upon returning home in the afternoon. In the past few months, a number of Palestinians have been shot in front of his family home, increasing the pressures on this child.*

Tougher Than Death

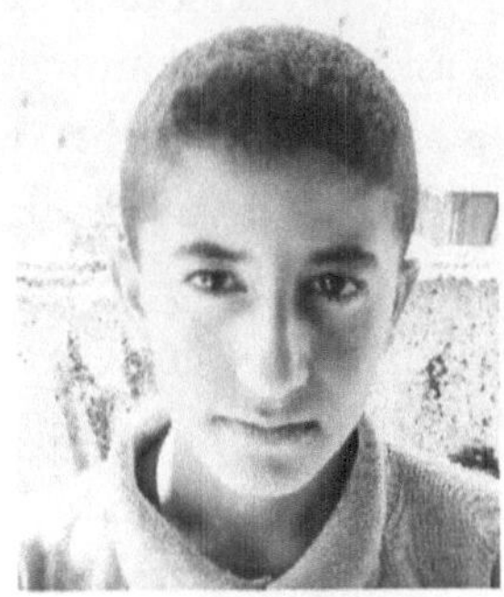

Mohammed Al-Khawaja
Age 11
Ramallah

I WAS a boy of 11 when the Occupation robbed me of my childhood and turned me into a young man who looks at life from a different perspective. I used to live in a world of childhood innocence, concerned with summer holidays, toys and new clothes.

I was a boy of 11 when the soldiers added me to the list of Palestinian prisoners whose names had never concerned me before, as I played my games. In the past, prisoners were just names to me, but after I was in jail, I knew mrore about their suffering as I experienced it first hand.

I will never forget the day my family's house was stormed. As the saying goes, children never forget. Dozens of soldiers filled our small house, which they turned into a military area. I never thought that our house would be frightening like this with so many soldiers and weapons. It never crossed my mind, even for a single second that I was the one who they were looking for, until they called out my name.

When the soldier asked for Mohammed, I was so terrified, my body shook. I wondered what they wanted from a boy of 11. The soldier who called my name handed me over to a group of soldiers, who looked like animals waiting for their food. They wore cruel smiles which revealed their hatred. I said goodbye to my family and I wished I didn't, because those moments were like a knife stabbing my body, every time I remembered them during my detention.

They took me from my home, leaving behind my dreams and my innocent life. I felt as if the lights had been turned off and the whole world had gone into darkness. I was severely beaten and hit by the soldiers all the way until we reached the village's entrance. I almost fainted. They were not satisfied with beating me, an innocent child, whose biggest pleasure until then was buying desserts and sweets. In the middle of the road, they grabbed me and threw me to the rough ground forcing me to crawl. I never stopped screaming and pleading for mercy, yet they paid no attention to my cries, and instead, became more cruel.

It was really tough for me, to the full extent of what the word tough means. I did not want to cry and let them enjoy seeing my tears falling down my cheeks, but I could not stop myself. I cried of sadness and oppression, of feeling unjustly treated and of innocence. I don't deny that I really felt scared and I recalled the images of my family, from the oldest to the youngest. I felt as if they were calling upon me. That scene of saying goodbye to them haunted me repeatedly.

My hands and those of the other boys, who were arrested under the charge of throwing stones, were handcuffed. They put us in a military vehicle then took us to an interrogation centre. Along the way, every time we whispered to each other, we were beaten and hurt. Five hours of interrogation felt like five months with all the psychological and physical pressure it entailed, in addition to the continuing beating by the soldiers. They left scars on our small bodies that told stories of pain and torture.

After the interrogation ended, I was moved to solitary confinement for the night, something I will never forget. I was alone there, suffering the nightmares of my own imagination and recalling the experiences of that day. In the midst of longing for my family, in pain and in tears, I felt even more alone when none of the jailers would respond to my requests of needing the toilet or giving me some water that would quench some of my thirst. That sad and cold night cannot be erased from my memory.

Next morning, we were transferred to Ofir Prison with my body still suffering in pain. I felt dead. I spent 14 days in that prison which was so hard for a boy of my age. Imprisonment was like death, or maybe even tougher. ♦

Israeli occupation forces crackdown on a peaceful protest in Nabi Saleh village which was organized to protest settlements and fired tear gas and assault children.

A Phone Call Changed My Life

Abdulrahman Adeli
Age 15
Nablus

EVERYONE knows about the harshness of the Occupation, but I had never experienced it, to its full extent, until I was arrested. I had heard many stories about how boys and men had been summoned by the Zionists, and imprisoned, but that didn't give me a hint of how the Occupation really treats us.

It was a sunny day and I had completed my homework quickly so I could go outside and play with my friends. I was about to leave the house, when a phone call to my father changed everything. A Zionist intelligence officer was on the line speaking to my father about one of his kids. I never thought it was me. I was just a kid who wanted to play and have fun.

My father put down the phone and looked confused and worried. I approached him and asked what was up. He looked at me sadly, put his head between his hands and let out a long sigh. The intelligence officer had asked my dad to take me to see them at one of the interrogation centres.

"I will never go and see them!" were my first words – I was furious at this absurd request. My father tried to calm me down because he knew it was not a simple matter. He sat me down next to him and asked me to think about it because the alternative was unknown and could be even worse.

The sun rose the next morning and I had not slept a single second, worried about what was going to happen to me. I kept comforting myself that I would not be arrested, for they could have taken me directly from my home, but they hadn't.

My father and I headed to the interrogation centre. As we approached I felt something telling me to stay away from that place. Nonetheless I tried to cling to the hope that I would not be arrested.

One of the officers came and asked my name. When I answered, he took my hand and told my father: *"We will return him in two days."* I was shocked. I knew that they were accusing me of something I hadn't done and instantly regretted not having listened to that voice inside me. My dad started pacing around, reciting prayers and looking very worried.

The soldiers handcuffed me and took me to another place and put me under arrest. I looked at my father for the last time before I was taken away, feeling so much pain in my heart. The way he looked at me made me even sadder. The situation was uncomfortable and almost made me cry, but I remained silent and resilient.

I was transferred to the interrogation centre where they left scars of torture on my body. They used threats and intimidation to achieve their goals and made me confess to baseless accusations under torture. They asked me about things I didn't know and people I had either never heard of, or rarely met. Every time I denied something, they would hit me and threaten me with worse things.

I spent five months in that dark prison where the sun could not be seen, and the moon could not light my summer nights.

Inside I laughed hysterically every time I remembered the false promises that they had made to me if I would confess. The jailers treated me badly throughout my imprisonment, as they tortured my soul. ♦

---

* *Abdulrahman quit school after he came out from prison as he could not catch up with his peers. He was unable to find a job so his father helped him start a small business. Later he was summoned with his brother by Israeli officers but was released after interrogation.*

Dreaming of Al-Aqsa

Abdulrahman Al-Araaj
Age 13
Qalandyia Refugee Camp

I ALMOST died of happiness when my father told me that he would take me to visit the Al-Aqsa Mosque, where Prophet Mohammed, peace be upon him, had ascended to the heavens. How beautiful to touch my forehead against its old stones and look at its main domes. From my family's house, which was once part of the Jerusalem district – but later got separated from it – I could almost hear the sound of the call to prayer at Al-Aqsa. Like other boys my age, I used to play in the yards of Al-Aqsa and would walk there with my friends. Nothing is more beautiful than having your soul and body unified in prayer there, at the place which was the original Qibla for Muslims.

I counted the days waiting for my next visit to Al-Aqsa.

That blessed Friday was the first Friday in the holy month of Ramadan. I woke at 6am, waiting for my father to give me the green light to start the journey. I had prepared myself for that day. I wore my best clothes as if I was going on holiday to a very special place. As we left the house, I told my father to hurry, gripping his hand, until we got into a taxi, which took us towards Jerusalem.

Israeli soldiers, armed-to-the-teeth, wearing cunning smiles, were waiting at Qalandyia military checkpoint. They abused Palestinians who wanted to cross. The hot sun increased the suffering of the Palestinians who were fasting that day. I was absent-minded, thinking of Al-Aqsa, only to be awakened by one of the soldiers, who called my name.

"Are you Abdulrahman?" one of the soldiers asked in a harsh tone. *"Yes,"* I nodded my head. He asked me to get out of the car. I didn't know that my beautiful dream of visiting Al-Aqsa was about to vanish. Surely this was a mistake. The soldier said something to my father, then grabbed my hand and threw me to the ground. My father started screaming at the soldiers, only to be pushed to the ground too as five more soldiers appeared out of nowhere.

Any belief in their humanity disappeared as the soldiers took me and threw me around between each other like a rag doll. They beat me all over my body. I was screaming and I could hear my father shouting at them. He tried to get through to help me, but they pushed him away.

These brutal soldiers left me for a while at the checkpoint, and then they took me along with my father to Almaskoubia interrogation centre. I had always wanted to enter Jerusalem, but not like this!

At the interrogation centre, they beat me again. I started bleeding and they left some scars on my body that remain today. The interrogator showed me photos of someone I didn't know, claiming that it was me. The interrogator was pressuring me to give him the names of boys from my refugee camp. Every time I didn't give him what he wanted, he would hit my face and head.

I was released that day, although it felt like I had experienced a decade of torture. I was bailed to return to a court hearing at some later date. A few weeks later, one of the military officers called my father, saying that they had not finished questioning me yet. They summoned me to the interrogation centre. If I didn't go I would be arrested and my family would be fined. I had to return for a second round of interrogation.

Despite my experiences in Jerusalem, I still long to visit Al-Aqsa. ◆

---

* *Abdulrahman resumed his schooling after his release, but 3 months later was rearrested. He is still in Israeli detention and has been informed he should expect to be sentenced to 15 months in prison and fined 3,000 NIS.*

* *Muslims originally prayed in the direction of Al-Aqsa. This changed to Mecca in 624 CE.*

Israeli soldiers arresting a Palestinian boy at Huwwarah checkpoint to the south of Nablus.

Rays of Freedom

Ahmed Badwan
Age 16
Jerusalem outskirts

I MIGHT be active and courageous and full of determination, but I can't stand chains. It's not that I'm a coward, it's because I was born free. So I want to live free and die free.

One day, my friend and I decided to go near an Israeli military checkpoint at the outskirts of my town. Here, the people of my town have tasted all sorts of pain and humiliation at the hands of Israeli soldiers, some of whom are barely 18 years of age. These young soldiers entertain themselves locking up Palestinians for no reason, at the checkpoint. Such degrading treatment was enough to spark anger in every single adult and child who all know that wretched place.

One day, my friend and I decided to do something. We walked towards the military checkpoint. We rushed into the area very quickly and threw stones at one of the soldiers, who was taken by surprise. I tried to run back to the area where I had come from, but I slipped and fell to the ground. My friend turned around to help me, but I screamed at him at the top of my voice telling him to leave.

He didn't know what to do. He was caught between the desire to help me and his instinct to flee from the soldiers coming to capture us. I saw soldiers approaching us from behind and I screamed at him again. I begged him to run away so that he would not get captured. He finally turned and ran. Shortly afterwards I was surrounded by many soldiers who beat every part of my body, until I felt numb.

I was barely alive when they transferred me to Atarout Military Centre. Worse was yet to come, as the interrogator threatened and terrorised me.

I was transferred to Ofir Prison where I was imprisoned for 35 days. It felt like years.

I felt bad, not because I had been arrested, but because I hated being imprisoned and not having my freedom.

I used to spend my time imagining myself free. I missed the sun, my family's house, my room and the souvenirs inside, and even looking at the photos in their frames. I visualised the faces of my family, and drew a smile, which equals my love for them in my heart. The longing for freedom inside me was unbelievable. I spent the long hours of waiting in prison indulging in a fantasy of living outside the prison.

The prison authorities increased my torment by refusing my family's requests to visit me, and denying me my right as a prisoner to buy items to make prison life more tolerable. All of this pressured me and pushed me towards the gate of the prison seeking freedom.

When the time to release me was due, I couldn't wait anymore. I collected my belongings and I raced outside, to the world, to the sunshine, to the shaking trees and the singing birds. I left the prison and went back to my family, and I crossed the same military checkpoint where I had been captured.

Passing through the checkpoint, I realised that the meaning of freedom was not what I had thought at all. It has a bigger and more beautiful meaning – freedom is when this checkpoint and its soldiers, military towers, wires, degradation and humiliation are gone. ♦

---

* *Ahmed never finished high school due to repeated absences when he was imprisoned. The lack of job opportunities in the West Bank has meant that he has been unable to find work, and this has made him severely depressed.*

My Family's House Became My Prison

Ahmed Salhab
Age 15
Jerusalem

I WAS approaching my home when the sound of the call to prayer reached my ears. It was a beautiful day in the holy month of Ramadan. I slowed my steps to listen to the Adhan.

I kept walking slowly on the narrow road looking at the houses, cobblestones and alleys. It was as if my heart was telling me that, one day, I would be deprived of the privilege of looking at them. I passed a group of boys playing football, who were kicking the ball so skillfully, it made me envious. I greeted one of the merchants as he was cleaning off the dust and sand from his shop's façade. My mind is full of memories about those beautiful and pleasant moments before that assault on me. At one particular moment I had been thinking of my family at our house, and of my mother preparing dinner and juice for us to break our fast. I was thinking of calling her to check if she needed any items for the house, when I heard a car approaching behind me. It came up alongside me, then crossed just in front of me. I didn't pay much attention to it at first, although I felt an uneasiness.

The car stopped and blocked my way. Soldiers in plain clothes and military vehicles appeared in front of me out of nowhere. They grabbed me and started beating me up. I felt blood coming out of my eyes and later I couldn't see anything. They took me to one of their vehicles as they continued beating and cursing me.

I was taken to the Almaskoubia Interrogation Centre to the west of Jerusalem. I had heard a lot of stories from friends and acquaintances about things that occurred here. The words and threats of interrogators were like arrows piercing my chest. Their fists hitting me caused vibrations of pain, which still resonate through my body.

I spent one week there, which felt like forever. I missed my house, my siblings and my mother. I tried to recall the time we had spent together in Ramadan, the delicious food, the laughter, and the interesting conversations which imprisonment had deprived me of – but the harsh reality of the prison awoke me from my beautiful dream.

Having my breakfast in prison was a horrible experience. Uncooked food was given to all of us despite the fact that we were fasting the whole day and desperately needed a piece of bread. After a week of imprisonment, I was released, but I was prevented returning to my home in the Mount of Olives, in Jerusalem. The decision to deport me was particularly tough as I had been longing to be at my house, spending time with my family in the last days of the holy month of Ramadan. Two months later, I was allowed to return to Jerusalem, but I was put under house arrest, which lasted until summer.

House arrest had a great impact on me. Had I been given the choice, I would have chosen to stay in prison, despite the bitterness of imprisonment, rather than being put under house arrest for a single day. House arrest deprives me of breathing fresh air and enjoying my childhood.

When I was eventually allowed to go back to school, one of my parents had to accompany me. After school I had to go back to my house and the doors were locked. My home turned into another prison for me, killing me a thousand times each day. ◆

---

* *Ahmed became a changed person after his imprisonment and house arrest. He missed interacting with his friends after school, as he had to go straight home. This devastated him and the pressure eventually made him quit school, since which he has been unable to work due to his security profile. He has to report to a police station every Monday.*

Alone In The Shadows

Amjad Qawwas
Age 15
Jerusalem

I WILL not feel ashamed of who I am for whatever reason.

I am a Palestinian who was taught, growing up, to love his country, and to love the wounded city of Jerusalem that is being taken over by the monsters of the Occupation from all directions.

The day started like any other day. I left the house with a group of my friends. We played football and talked for a while. We had no plans, other than playing football and talking to each other.

All of a sudden, I heard screams and explosions which changed the course of that day. My friends and I ran towards the direction of the noise where we saw Israeli soldiers and police firing gas canisters and explosives at the houses in our neighbourhood. Down the road, we saw a number of young people defending themselves – throwing stones and fireworks.

The clashes lasted for hours and many people were injured, beaten and arrested. I was one of them as I got caught with some other kids by a special unit of soldiers disguised in plain clothes. Every single inch of my body was beaten. I bled, but I didn't care. I had to act like a grown-up, even though I was only a teenager.

I was moved to a nearby settlement built on the stolen land of Souwana, where soldiers continued beating, humiliating, and demonstrating their hatred for me. I wanted to cry, but I didn't want to show them I was in pain, and let them think I was weak. Although by world standards I am considered a child, Jerusalem's children are forced to become adults by this Occupation.

I was taken by military van to a police station. Zionists claim that they respect the law. This is not true! I was interrogated for two hours and then I was taken to Almaskobuia Detention Centre where the real suffering began.

I spent 20 days there. The jailors purposely placed me in solitary confinement. Some people might say it's not difficult to bear. I had heard about solitary confinement but I hadn't paid attention to what was said. Now after experiencing it, let me tell you that it is a prison inside a prison – an endless sort of darkness.

I was put in a cell, which was almost as small as I was. There was nothing there except for very weak lighting. I kept looking at the walls and the roof of the cell, trying to measure its size, as if I was preparing my body to live there. I wondered how I could live here for days. I tried to occupy myself with something, anything, but it was far from easy. There was literally nothing to do.

I sat on the ground. My imagination took me to our big house and to my family. I closed my eyes and there I was, sitting in our yard, under the trees. I reached my hands out to touch the grapes and the olive leaves in my family's garden. Instead, I felt the walls of that damned cell. I closed my eyes again and tried to imagine something beautiful, but then I heard a sound next to me, rising in volume. I opened my eyes to find an army of insects invading my cell.

I will never forget how much I suffered during those two days in solitary confinement. That cell will never be erased from my memory. Now I feel pain whenever I think of other child prisoners who are there, wondering how they will survive. Those people were born free and will never accept injustice. I was released and deported to my grandfather's house, where I was put under house arrest, until further notification. This was much worse than solitary confinement!

♦

---

* *After his release, Amjad was placed under house arrest at his grandfather's house for one year. Although he was allowed to attend school, he failed in the year he was arrested. The whole experience has deeply affected him and he is unable to sleep well and interact with his friends anymore.*

A Revolutionary Spirit

Ammar Adeli
Age 14
Nablus

I GRABBED the remote control and switched between the channels looking for a cartoon program. When surfing the channels, I came to a scene of a young man wearing a mask, standing proudly, holding stones and looking at the Israeli soldiers, in a challenging manner, without fear. He had collected stones and was throwing them at the soldiers, as if he was throwing blocks of fire. I gazed at him and observed his moves. I imagined myself standing next to him.

Since then, I had a special place in my heart for the stone-throwers. I wanted to see them close-up. I started dreaming of seeing one of them going past me. I looked up to them as heroes, and it gave me, an 11-year-old-boy living under a humiliating occupation, some strength. I started thinking like the adults, cursing the situation which led us to this stage. I was full of rebellion, inspired by that young man wearing a mask, whose eyes were full of hope for freedom.

One night, as I was about to go to bed, I heard the sounds of explosions and screams in our village. I looked from the window and saw lights and heard the sound of bombs. I knew immediately that there were clashes at the village's

main entrance. I closed the curtains and went back to my bed. I imagined that masked man again standing in front of me, calling me. For a minute I felt an internal conflict. But then I decided to put on my jacket and go outside, towards the direction of the clashes.

I insisted on participating in our Palestinian struggle. It was not just a game to me, but rather a cause, much older than I was.

I collected some stones and threw them at the Occupation soldiers, with the image of that young man still haunting me, pushing me to accept that challenge. I spent a few hours there, but then two soldiers, with the help of military training, captured this little boy who was throwing stones at them for the first time.

They started cursing and beating me. Then they handed me over to one of the coordination centres run by the Palestinian Authority. They were satisfied with that initial punishment, but it was not the end of the story.

By the time I was 14, the anger inside me had mounted, and I looked at the Occupation as something that I should face with all my strength. I participated many times in the clashes at the entrance of my village and later I was arrested for a second time. This time, I was transferred to Huwara detention centre. I had my share of beatings and assaults, which made my hands and head bleed, yet I didn't fulfil the interrogators' dream of seeing me cry, nor showing fear of their power.

I was interrogated for 20 days, after which I was sentenced to two months in Megiddo Prison. It was a very tough experience, which shaped my character and strengthened the spirit of resistance inside me, which many boys my age lacked.

Despite the imprisonment, I did not lose my determination to resist the Occupation. So 40 days later, I started throwing stones again. The soldiers had photos of me and they were looking for me. I was so proud that although I was only a boy of 14, they felt threatened by me.

I was arrested for the third time and I was exposed again to all their bloody tactics of torture, such as beating and sleep deprivation. I spent several months in prison again, but the image of that young man with a mask continued to inspire me even when I was in chains. ♦

---

* *After repeated arrests, Ammar could not keep up with school so he quit. He has not been able to find work due to high unemployment in the West Bank. His relationship with his family has suffered.*

Israeli soldiers arresting a Palestinian boy at Huwwarah checkpoint to the south of Nablus.

The Night the Shabak** Came

Ayman Abbasi
Age 16
Jerusalem

MANY events in my life occupy my memory even though I am still a child according to international norms. They are not necessarily beautiful memories, some are good, some are bad and some provide me with a glimmer of hope.

I was in 9th grade when I was imprisoned for the first time. I don't like to talk about that dark night, but I must. It was a night I won't forget for as long as I live. Loud knocks sounded at my family's front door. My mother's screams and my siblings' tears are two things that will stay with me forever. These memories attempt to create a state of tension inside me, but I try to forget about them.

I was shocked at the force the Israeli security apparatus used on me at my family's home in Jerusalem's Raas Alamoud neighbourhood. The moment I was arrested I expected to be beaten. However at the interrogation centre, I was hit so badly in the face, that when my family saw me at court, they could barely recognise me because of the marks and bruises.

I was really uneasy about not being able to go to school. I was constantly worried in the prison, thinking of my own desk in the class and my classmates in the school. I thought many times of what would happen to me and to my studies and how I would manage if I continued to be detained.

After 14 days at Almaskoubia interrogation centre I was released, and was relieved that I would be going back to school. However I was then served with an open-ended sentence under house arrest. I felt like screaming at the judge and telling him that returning me to prison would be better than this sort of torture. I was under house arrest for 10 months – it felt like years. I stared from my window every morning at the kids going to school carrying their bags, while I languished imprisoned at home.

I missed many details which I had never paid attention to before I was arrested. I missed the school bell, the guard's face, and the morning queue. How I longed to queue like all of the other kids. I didn't know that I would long for a life full of those things that I had not appreciated before.

I was not allowed to see my friends or talk to them. I was not allowed to go to school. I was not allowed to do anything. Were they able, they would have prevented me from breathing. After 10 months of house arrest, the court sentenced me to 18 more months in prison, so I had to hand myself over to the prison authorities again.

I served the sentence at Hasharon prison. Words can't describe the situation there. It looked like a grave, full of boys and teenagers from every city, village and refugee camp. The room we were in had stories written on its walls by former inmates, covered with dust. Boys acted like men and except for age, there was no distinction between them and adults.

I will never forget the day when forces from the Israeli Prison Service stormed our cell. They turned it upside down and searched every single item. They stole our belongings which we used to entertain ourselves in that horrible prison. They even stole my headphones, which I used to listen to the radio in an attempt to forget my misery.

The prison was cold, with no blankets. We never felt warm there. Despite this, there was always hope on the boys' faces. I didn't realise how much I missed freedom until I was released. ♦

---

* *On 29 November 2015, Israeli soldiers shot and killed Ayman during a clash at Ein al Louza. They even attempted, albeit unsuccessfully, to seize*

his body from the medical centre where he had been taken. At midnight, hundreds of Palestinians accompanied Ayman's body to the graveyard in Sweih, carrying flags and chanting for the liberation of Palestine and the release of all detainees. May Allah place him among the martyrs.

** *Shabak is the Hebrew word for the Shin Bet — the Israeli counterintelligence and internal security force.*

Ramadan in Prison

Baraa' Abushama
Age 16
Ramallah

I WANTED to stay up late for I didn't want to wake up early in Ramadan. Yet, sleep came over me by midnight. During my slumber, I had nightmares and confusing dreams. I woke up to find out that it was only 4am, and the Fajr Prayer was still two hours away. I sipped some water and went back to sleep.

Minutes later, I thought I heard monsters knocking on our front door. I rubbed my eyes, got up quickly and stood still behind my bedroom door, waiting for someone from my family to open the door. The soldiers who were knocking didn't wait for us to open the door

– they broke in. They stormed the house and turned it upside down.

My pulse was racing. I knew in my heart that the soldiers were here to arrest me, as they had carried out a number of similar raids in the village throughout the last two weeks. They transformed our beautiful house into a heap of furniture, papers and clothes. They asked my mother about me, She quickly responded: *"He is a little child who doesn't even have an ID card."* The soldier asked her to stop talking.

The same soldier asked me to come to him. I followed his instruction, trying to show I didn't care although I was worried inside. Images came to my mind of Eid visits, Ramadan banquets, having Sohour with my family, and the call to prayer. I imagined that all of these things would disappear from my life this year.

I started imagining what would happen to me. Where would they take me in that night of Ramadan? Would I spend Eid with my family or not?

The soldiers handcuffed me as they cursed me and took me from my family to their vehicles parked outside. I could hear my mother reciting prayers for my safety, and it made me feel sad. They transferred me to a military checkpoint at the entrance of our village. I was placed on the floor, still blindfolded and tightly bound. Then they took me to Sha'ir Benjamin, where I was put in a very small room, alone for five hours.

The plastic ties were pressing so hard against my veins, I was afraid that they were going to explode. From time to time, I tried to move my hands so as not to feel numb.

I was fasting and was trying to avoid any feelings of thirst. When we talk about the Occupation, nothing is surprising. Soldiers were eating and drinking in front of us, increasing our suffering and trying to push us to surrender. But, thanks to God, we were not affected much.

I was chained until I arrived at the interrogation centre. My interrogator's body was huge. He was well-built and looked at us kids in a terrifying manner, trying to frighten us and make us confess, whether or not we had committed any crime. In a harsh voice, he asked me if I had thrown Molotov cocktails at settlers' cars. I denied it. He kept asking me the same thing for many hours. During that time, I was cursed and psychologically tortured.

I was held until 8pm that day although I was fasting and was feeling thirsty and hungry. They subjected me to humiliation. I was asking them for water, but they refused to give me any. My head started to ache and I was so tired I almost fell down.

They took us to the gate of Ofir Prison and released me along with a number of boys. One of the soldiers released me from chains after 17 hours of imprisonment.

Prior to releasing me. a soldier intentionally cut my arm with his razor. I felt my body shaking, not because they were so powerful, but because the feeling of oppression was so great. My only solace is that I will grow up one day. It was a short day for many, but for me, it had been the longest day of my life. ♦

---

* *Despite the harsh experiences he has been through, Baraa' has managed to continue his education, and is currently in 12th Grade. However this experience has changed him and made him nervous and irritable with his loved ones.*

Roses and Guns

Malak Al-Khatib
Age 14
Ramallah

THE day was calm, filled with the early scent of spring. I could hardly wait to finish my exams and leave school, as I wanted to enjoy the spring day, walking back to my family's house. The beauty of nature was reflected in my answers to the exam questions. My village was like a bride dressed in green.

I spent the last moments looking at the growing buds from my class window. I was impatient because of my love for the land, which is mixed with passion and warmth. When the bell rang, I quickly left the class and when walking home, I noticed rows of roses growing by the path.

Although I needed to be home for lunch with my family who were waiting for me, I lingered among the flowers because time means nothing in a child's mind.

As I wandered around picking the flowers, I suddenly realised that I had reached a place that I had never been to before. The beauty of the scene though was stronger than me. I heard the sounds of vehicles driving across the main road, which led to an illegal Zionist settlement, near to my village, but I didn't pay attention to them. I was busy enjoying my land, in my village, in my homeland.

Suddenly I heard shouts, which terrified me and made the beautiful roses fall from my hands. A group of soldiers, armed-to-the-teeth, appeared in front of me, and pointed their guns at me.

Although I had committed no crime, they grabbed me, chaining my hands and blindfolding me. The soldiers picked me up like booty they had won after fighting a war, and threw me inside one of their military vehicles. They cursed and assaulted my little body and ended my childish thoughts of roses and breezes.

I was transferred to one of the interrogation centres where they repeatedly threatened me. I had enough strength to neither cry or show weakness in front of them. They fabricated a charge against me of throwing stones at their military vehicles. Is this their dictionary's interpretation of wandering in nature, because they are so obsessed with security?

I denied all of the charges. I was later taken to Hasharon Prison where female prisoners are held. I walked into prison feeling I was walking into a dark grave, with many bodies simply striving to stay alive. The female prisoners were surprised to see me but they could understand, from their experience, how a child simply walking among the roses could be arrested.

I spent about two months with them. I was released and my heart was still full of sorrow, not because I was arrested, but rather because of the injustice Palestinians are still facing. I still have so much sorrow in my heart, because the darkness in our lives has not yet come to an end, and we, the victims, are still struggling on the path to freedom. ♦

---

* *Malak now suffers panic attacks in the night whenever she dreams about her arrest and imprisonment. She is going through a difficult time due to her family's financial difficulties and is upset about the lack of interest by the Palestinian Authority in her case.*

A Palestinian family is trying to set their little boy free from the hands of an Israeli soldier in the West Bank's village of Nabi Saleh to the north west of Ramallah.

Don't Be Sad if I Get Arrested

Mohammed Abuatwan
Age 15
Hebron

I CLOSED my book and put it inside my bag. I went to bed, feeling tired and exhausted, as I had woken up early that morning. I placed my head on my pillow and smiled as I recalled events that had happened during the day, as I always did every night.

I fell asleep quickly, feeling tired after having played football and studied with my friends. I had slept barely a few hours when I was awakened by knocks on the door. At first, I thought I was dreaming, and that it was our neighbour knocking on the door, to realise otherwise later.

I got up from my bed and walked towards my bedroom door while still hoping that I was dreaming. Any hopes I had were dashed when I saw my entire family running towards me. Minutes later, we heard the sounds of explosions. We threw ourselves to the ground and kept our heads down. When we stood up again and looked towards the door, we saw a military convoy moving like thunder in every direction as they stormed the house.

When I realised it was Israeli Occupation soldiers, I felt less scared as it was not the first time that they had invaded our home. I thought they were searching for someone, or maybe just wanted to turn everything upside down – nothing more. They turned the house into a total mess, smashing our belongings as they moved us from one room to another. All I wanted was for them to leave our house so that I could get some sleep. Yet, I was surprised to hear them repeating my name.

"Who is Mohammed?" a soldier shouted. I answered with a weak tone: *"It's me."* He looked down at me, not expecting that I would be this small and young. He double-checked my identity with my father who showed him some documents. Only then was he sure that I was Mohammed whose name is registered in my father's ID card. *"Follow me,"* he said.

These two words changed the course of my life. I didn't expect that the whole raid, which entailed searches, and so much brutality, was designed to capture me, a boy of 15. I looked at my family's faces as I had so many questions, but I could find no answers, leaving me in a state of shock. My father tried to protest, only to be kicked by one of the soldiers. *"Don't feel worried about him,"* said one of the soldiers with a sarcastic smile.

A new part in my life started at that moment. I was handcuffed and blindfolded and taken to their military vehicles. I was in total disbelief. Was I dreaming or was it a strange new reality? Had I become a number in the prisoners' record, which I had often heard about? Many questions swirled in my mind for a while until a soldier hit me. It was the first time I got hit but it was not the last, and it was probably the least harmful. He hit me again and again as if I was behind the bombing of Tel Aviv, and they were punishing me for doing that!

I was transferred to a military centre near Hebron where I tasted all sorts of torture, beating and humiliation. I felt blood dripping down my nose and mouth, but I could not raise my hands to the wounds, as I was handcuffed. My little body turned into a map of pain, compared to their huge bodies which I imagined as ghosts.

After I was released, I constantly feared being arrested again. That night changed my life a lot and my name became listed among those classified as "wanted" and "terrorists." I have since been arrested again and held for a few days. Nowadays, before I go to bed,

I tell my parents *"Don't be sad if I get arrested again tonight."* ♦

---

* *Mohammed was rearrested a month after he was released, and sentenced to five months imprisonment and fined 3,000 NIS. Due to repeated arrests, he dropped out of school and opted for vocational training. Despite obtaining a diploma in car mechanics, he has been unable to find work and this has affected him psychologically.*

Israeli soldiers patrolling Alshuhada Street in Hebron to protect Israeli settlers residing there.

Tortured Memories

Saleh Khader
Age 16
Hebron

IMPRISONMENT is tough and bitter for everyone. It is the case with my own experience too, but I also feel proud that I survived it. I sit on my bed every day trying to remember the tiny details of my life in prison.

Until I was arrested, I didn't realise that going to prison left serious psychological and physical impacts on prisoners. I used to think that people who get arrested are handcuffed and blindfolded at most. Perhaps I even desired to be arrested, for I knew that prisoners were treated as heroes.

One day, as often happened, two of my friends invited me to go for a walk in the village. Something that day had told me to wear my good shoes and thick shirt. We walked along the village streets, and then we reached a narrow road. It was new, but in our naivety, we thought nothing of it, and continued walking.

Suddenly, one of my friends shouted, *"Army! Army!"* I looked around and at first I saw no one. They were extremely cunning. Suddenly, dozens of soldiers surrounded us. They had been hiding behind some trees. They divided themselves into groups; each group tasked to capture one of us. They left scars on our bodies as they assaulted us.

I was beaten and kicked all over. The attacks on my body seemed to last for years. I wished they would take me to their military vehicle, at least they would stop beating me there. From the screams of my other two friends, I knew we were all treated the same by those Zionists, who seemed to only know hatred.

They never stopped cursing us. The beatings would leave its scars on our young bodies, rooting this painful memory in our minds forever. Finally, the journey of pain ended, or at least that is what I thought. We were taken by military jeep to Gosh Atsyoun Detention Centre where we were held for a few hours. Later, we were taken to Kiryat Arba'a Police Centre, where something took place, which I will never forget.

They took us to a darkened room. We could hardly see anything. The three of us were extremely tired, our bodies were exhausted and bruised from all the beatings. Out of the darkness, a soldier appeared and asked us about teenagers and young men from our village, who he claimed threw stones at the vehicles and cars of settlers. We knew none of them, and even if we had, we would not know if they participated in throwing stones or not.

Of course, none of our answers satisfied the interrogator. He came closer and punched me hard in my eye and jaw. At first, I thought he had smashed it. Blood started flowing out from my mouth and I felt myself boiling with rage. He approached my friend and repeated the question. My friend didn't answer, so he hit him in his face even harder. It continued like this for some time. He asked, we didn't answer, and then he hit us again.

Another interrogator entered the room carrying something in his hand, which looked unfamiliar to me. I didn't pay attention to him at the beginning until I saw him connecting an electric wire to the wall and then he started walking towards us, carrying that tool. I didn't know what it was, but I knew it was used for torture, so I closed my eyes waiting for more pain to come. My friend screamed in a way I never heard him screaming before. I opened my eyes to realize that he was being electrocuted, a boy of 15 screaming for help. How could I help him while I was still handcuffed? I was barely able to move. He was screaming, and every time he did, my body would shake and my heart would run faster. For a while, I thought my heart would stop as a result of feeling so angry but helpless. Despite this, I held my tears back and didn't show them to the interrogators.

It was a tragic night in my childhood. I was transferred to Ofir Prison after a day of beatings and torture. My friend's screams were stuck in my mind. Every time I remember this horrific incident, I close my eyes. I still have tears inside my heart, from that one day in their detention centre. ♦

Arrested for the 15th Time!

Muslim Ouda
Age 13
Jerusalem

IT was a calm night and I had been laughing with my family. We heard military vehicles and my father jokingly asked: *"How many times would you have been arrested if you got arrested tonight?"* I told him with a smile, *"I'm not sure — 14 or 15."*

Prison had left its scars on me as I had been arrested many times before that night, even though I was less than 13 years old. This time, it was a group of Israeli soldiers in plain clothes that attacked and detained me. They beat me and I screamed in pain. One of them hit me in the eye with a sharp tool which caused a fracture in my skull.

Despite my young age, the prison made me act like a grown man. I didn't fear the Zionists or being arrested. Yes, I would miss my family, my house and my friends, but despite the miserable conditions in the cells, I would still try to draw a bright picture of my future, using my innocent imagination, one in which there was no Occupation.

I was taken during that arrest to several interrogation centres where Israeli officers swore and screamed at me. Then they took me out of the interrogation rooms, which were full of surveillance equipment and beat and humiliated me. Every time I was arrested, they would treat me even harsher, as they knew how resilient I was. They unleashed the hatred from their hearts against me.

At court, it was even more painful. It's true that I wasn't beaten in front of the judge or the lawyers and I would feel so thrilled to see my family. But seeing my family would also bring enormous pain to my heart. I missed them so much. Police officers in the court would not allow us to communicate, shake hands or even make gestures. I cursed the jailors and the prison so many times for depriving me of being with them.

In the prison's cells, I would sit on the ground, putting my head between my knees, trying to use my imagination to take me to my own world away from imprisonment, interrogation and rotten food. I would travel to Albustan neighbourhood, where my family lives, imagining its narrow aisles and old houses. I imagined myself kicking a football with my friend. I imagined myself entering my home, smelling the delicious food my mother cooked, throwing myself on my bed and sleeping for long hours to be awakened by my mother's caring voice. I imagined a life that was not spoiled by arrests or assassinations, by military units in plain clothes.

There were many times I would be put under house arrest for charges that I had nothing to do with. It was like the judge was a character in a play designed to take revenge on Jerusalem's children. I spent long weeks and months under house arrest, which restricted my thinking as well as movement. Actual imprisonment is less harmful than that slow death which Jerusalem's children are subjected to in their homes.

Prison is a place I hate because it made me miss a lot of my education. I don't think it will be the last time I get arrested, as my name has become very familiar in their records and they want to take my love of Jerusalem from my heart. ♦

---

* *Muslim Ouda was arrested three more times after conducting this interview and has now been arrested 18 times, although he is barely 14 years old.*

An Israeli solider blocking the way of a Palestinian boy at Alshuhada Street in Hebron.

The Coldness in My Bones

Waseem Abumaria
Age 14
Hebron

ALTHOUGH it was a rainy day, I chose to go outside the house rather than staying inside observing the drops of rain, slowly falling down the glass. I was bored and thought I would visit my grandparents as being with them is a lot of fun and they are always happy for me to visit.

I only put on a light coat as their house is not that far away. I walked along wondering what I would do there on this rainy day. Just like any other child, I stepped over my shadow and of course jumped over all the puddles on my way.

I heard a weird sound which stopped me in my tracks. Suddenly I felt something poking into my back. It was the gun of an Israeli soldier. I had fallen into a trap. I was shocked. Yes, it had been designed to catch this 14 year old boy. At that moment, my memories flashed in front of my eyes, as I tried to figure why they had caught me. Had they mistaken me for someone else?

Regardless of my innocence, the soldiers treated me harshly. They took me to one of the parks nearby and transferred me to other military personnel who handcuffed me and took me in a convoy to a nearby settler colony. They made serious threats against me, in the hope that I would confess to something I hadn't done.

The weather got colder and it rained heavily, but this time the rain was not as interesting to me as it had been on my way to my grandparents' house. I refused to confess to anything. They kept me in the rain which made my clothes wet. The coldness got into my bones. I stayed like this for an hour and they ignored my pleas for mercy. Whilst they were arranging my transfer to an interrogation centre, they put me in a room, where I was screamed at, threatened and beaten again. I spent 18 days in Gosh Atsyoun Detention Centre, before I was released.

The cold winds were blowing when I was released from prison. A part of me has remained in those prison cells as I feel for the suffering of prisoners during the wintry days.

When I saw my family after that first separation, their faces were more beautiful, and their words nicer, and everything seemed to be lighter than before, because now I knew the value of freedom. We walked quickly away from the detention centre. I felt my heart beating fast, telling me not to forget the other prisoners, who did not know the date of their own freedom. ♦

---

* *Waseem was rearrested in October 2015, and this time he was beaten so severely it affected his health. He was released a month later and fined 1,000 NIS. The Israeli court is still investigating him, and while he is*

waiting for a final decision, he has returned to school where he is studying in Grade 10. Waseem experiences nightmares from time to time, where he wakes up screaming after reliving his prison experiences

Rotten Food

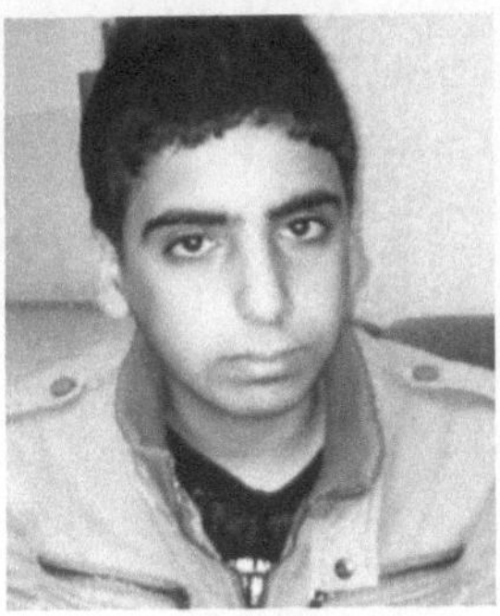

Ahmed Khalaf
Age 13
Jenin

I SAW myself walking in green fields, laughing with my family members, with my father making tea and my mother offering us sweets, then I woke to an unpleasant sound which didn't let me finish my beautiful dream.

It was the voice of one of the soldiers demanding that we stand in a queue so they could count the prisoners, as they did every morning. This was our daily programme, here in the graves of the living. Each day, I woke up early and stood in that queue, just to pass time. I waited for the evening count and then I would go to sleep. Sleeping allowed me to dream of the three most important things in my life: home, family and school.

Every hour of every day, I recalled what happened to me that day when I was captured by the monsters of the Occupation. Nothing seemed unusual as my friend and I went to one of the parks in our village to celebrate the end of our final exams. As we were enjoying the beauty of the scenery and nature, we heard the sound of a military vehicle driving towards us. We ran away and tried to hide from it, but the vehicle was faster than us 13 year old boys.

I didn't think that imprisonment would be our destiny as we had committed no crime, apart from enjoying the scenery in the park. I really thought that they had some humanity, but I was wrong. They chased and caught us and then ordered us to take off our clothes. They put us against the wall of their military vehicle and tortured us, leaving scars all over our backs.

They then transferred us to the military checkpoint at Al-Jalamieh where we were subjected to assaults and humiliations for hours and hours. Next, they took us for interrogation, which reminded us of what we had seen in movies, but which we had thought only existed in fiction. But it was a reality that is now etched in our memories -the ugliest pictures. The interrogator tried to scare me, but I faced him with courage. He was screaming at me trying to humiliate me. I screamed back at him louder than he did. He got a stick and beat me and kicked me, until I felt like I was dead. The world closed in on me and my life was ending. Even after that chapter of suffering had ended, I was still in pain for another two months, due to the severity of their attacks.

The jailers served me food on the toilet floor. I would quickly start eating because I was starving and tired. In my family, I used to decide what my mother would cook. Here I was forced to eat food which I didn't know what its ingredients were. They served us rotten food, something I worked out after suffering severe stomach pains.

Longing for the three important things in my innocent life was killing me. Every day, I recalled the features of every single member of my family, as if I was asking my mind to help me memorise them. Their features were fading in my memory so I had to exert extra effort. I needed to keep them, because they were my only sources of hope in that scary prison.

I was transferred to Megiddo prison where I was sentenced to six months in prison. My father paid some money so that I would be released on bail after serving half of the sentence. I served three months waiting for freedom and fresh breezes of air which were absent in our dark cells. Once I was out, I knew that I would be happy for every moment I was free. ♦

---

* *Ahmed had trouble catching up with lessons after his release, and quit school. However, he has not been able to get a job either and the sense of failure has affected him psychologically. His family worries about him.*

Israeli special forces arrest a Palestinian boy during clashes at Bit Eil to the north of Ramallah.

Punished For Protesting

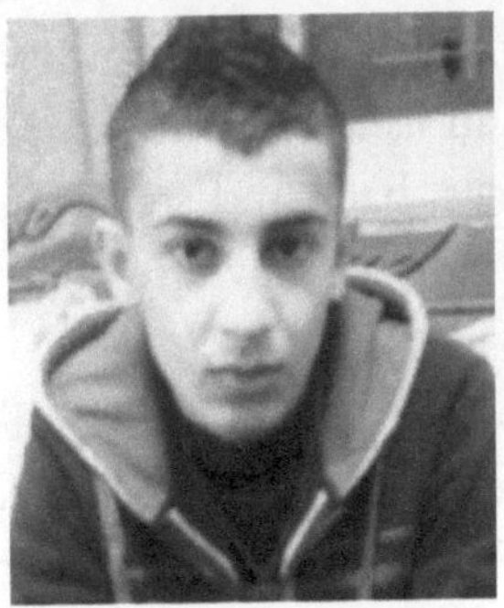

Alaa' Hinthawi
Age 17
Jenin

I WISH that I had been arrested at my home. At least, they would have treated me better in front of my family. Instead, I was arrested while taking part in a protest of solidarity with Palestinian hunger-striker Samer Issawi. It was a very tough experience for me, where I was subjected to all forms of humiliation, assault and deprivation.

I took part in the protest, not just because my friends did, but because I felt responsible towards my people, even though I was barely 17 years old. I felt it was my duty as a Palestinian and that Issawi would be stronger and more resilient with people like me standing in solidarity with him.

The protest was about to come to an end when I was captured by some Israeli soldiers whom I had thrown stones at. They chased me, but I could not escape. I was like a deer hunted by wolves.

The way they captured me reminded me of wildlife programmes that I used to watch. They hit me with their guns, sticks, feet and fists. They held my legs and arms, and struck my head, face, back and stomach. I felt I was going to faint from the pain as they stretched my body close to breaking point.

I was left outdoors, in the rain. I felt like vomiting due to the cold and the beating I had been subjected to. Later, they transferred me to Aljalamieh military checkpoint where they tried to force me to confess to many things I hadn't done, like shooting a gun.

They told me to sign papers in Hebrew which they claimed would help me get released. I felt doubtful about their promises. Why would they be helping me, when it was they who had arrested me? I refused to sign. Later, I learnt that those papers were an admission of guilt to the trumped up charges.

I was transferred to Megiddo prison where I experienced first hand the suffering and pain of prisoners. The living conditions were miserable. Could these jailors actually have kids who they kiss and tell beautiful stories to before going to sleep? I could not believe that the soldiers who assaulted me had children whom they cared about.

I spent a few months in prison. I got bored of eating cans of tuna and corn, which were our only food. I missed my mother's cooking and its delicious smell that wafted throughout our home, attracting us to the kitchen. I thought about my life before and how I used to complain about trivial issues.

Now, I feel more optimistic and hopeful. The meaning of freedom has a greater significance in my dictionary of my life because the Occupation wants us to feel hopeless and never realise the importance of freedom. ♦

Spring of Suffering

Osaid Abubaker
Age 14
Jenin

IT was a beautiful spring day. The smell of roses entered my senses and the warm breezes of air danced around me, leading me to another world, with no modern buildings, or air pollution from cars driving on paved roads, organised in a disturbing manner.

I was 14 and all I cared about was having fun without restrictions, not having to worry about time or any form of organisation. I loved walking in green fields. I had been waiting for winter to end so I could see the land flourishing in colour, after its watering by the rains. It was now March and I planned to visit some land that my family owned near an Israeli settler colony, which had been built on the lands of my village.

I brought my friend with me, thinking it would be an interesting day that we would remember. The noise of the military vehicles that we heard as we got close to the colony meant it would be, but for a very different reason. The soldiers chased and then captured us. We were boys running away from soldiers who were armed to the teeth.

They tied up our hands and took us inside the colony, where a group of them battered us to the edge of death. They didn't regard us as humans, let alone children. We received kicks and beatings all over our bodies and we screamed for help at the top of our voices, but our calls were unanswered.

The soldiers left us with the ugliest memories in our minds as they pressured us to confess to throwing stones at the colony, but we refused. I kept asking myself: *"Is it illegal to walk to and visit the land my family owns? Why was I deprived of enjoying the fresh air of spring which I longed for? Do I need a permit to be able to move in my land, in my village and in my country?"*

Their beating stopped me from continuing to ask those questions. I felt so much pain – my body was broken. We were then transferred to Megiddo prison. Using threats against us is how the Occupation tries to make us afraid and push us to confess to things that we haven't done. They made their threats clear: torture; deprivation of everything; and imprisonment for years. Their threats affected us seriously, being children, and brought pain and apprehension to our hearts.

In Megiddo prison we saw the true suffering of prisoners. Nothing was good there. Nothing. Food was not good. The whole place was not good. There were armies of insects everywhere. How beautiful insects were, when they were in the green fields and how ugly they were in those dirty cells.

I had gone through difficult times and I was in so much pain. I suffered from flu and had some other diseases, but all they gave me were pain killers. No one listened to me in the so-called prison 'clinic'. I wondered what might have happened to me if I had suffered from a serious illness. I was released three months later. I still think about it. Spring was spoiled by the snakes of the Occupation and just thinking about it now makes me feel worried that I might be arrested again! ♦

---

* *Osaid went back to school after he was released, but shortly after, was rearrested and sentenced to 5 years in prison, where he remains today.*

A boy besing arrested during a protest in the village of Iraq Bureen to the South of Nablus.

They Stole My Sight

Saleh Rodwan
Age 14
Qalqeilia

I WOKE from my sleep worried, as a tear rolled down my cheek. I opened and rubbed my eyes, but I could not see as usual. I touched the edge of the bed and tried to walk forward hoping to regain my vision. I walked towards the door of the cell, then made my way back to my bed.

Since my imprisonment, I have been living in a complex world, dominated by the senses of weakness and sickness. Every day when I woke up I felt like this, as I tried to recall the beautiful memories of home, while the memories of the day when I was arrested overwhelmed me, reminding me of the expression on my family's faces, even though I had not been able to see them well.

It had been a normal day. I had no inkling of anything that was about to happen. I went to sleep, feeling tired, but was awoken by knocks on our front door. It was not the first time the Zionists had raided our house, as my brothers have been arrested before. But this was the first time that they had come looking for me, a boy of 14.

When a soldier called my name, I felt something moving inside me, making me feel angry and sad at the same time.

I controlled myself, understanding the seriousness of the situation. I knew they had come to arrest me. The soldiers took me to their military vehicles, and then drove me to a detention centre. They interrogated me claiming that I had participated in throwing stones and smashing settlers' cars, near my town, Azzoun.

I wasn't too worried because my brothers and friends who have been arrested before had given me the necessary knowledge to deal with the situation. In the interrogation room, I saw all sorts of torture and humiliation. If an Israeli child was exposed to it, I am sure that the whole world would shake with anger. I tried to be patient waiting for my own destiny.

I was sentenced to two years in prison, which I served at Megiddo prison. Imprisonment was not my first concern, for as the saying goes "prisons are for men." I did however experience worsening pain in my eye, from a problem I had had earlier in my childhood. The jailers ignored my pleas as well as those of other prisoners for assistance, which I considered medical negligence.

I spent days crying in pain. I began to lose the ability to see things clearly, even objects close to me. I felt the bitterness of the prison and the suffering of deprivation and realised the jailers' ability to show their toughness, regardless of the justification. It was as if they found in my illness an opportunity to increase my pain. Every time I shouted for medication they would laugh and make fun of me. I reminded them that I was a child, but I got no response, which made me feel even more desperate.

Before I was captured I used to receive medical care at a hospital in Jerusalem. I had not finished the course of medicines which I had been prescribed. Throughout my two years of imprisonment I asked for my medication several times, but I was not given any. Eventually, those rejections caused the loss of my sight

I was alone in the prison struggling with my illness, writing imaginary letters of anger. I wished the pain could go away without medication so that I could beat the jailer and his cruel sarcasm. I wished that I was a normal boy with no illness and no visual problems so I could serve my sentence without showing any weakness. I felt so much oppression, completely powerless facing an army of terror. I wished so much to lie on my mother's lap, so that she could wipe away my sadness with her love, and place a kiss on my forehead as she always used to do. ♦

---

* *Saleh had to drop out of school after he was released, due to his inability to catch up with his classmates. Soon afterwards, his brother Mohammed was shot in the legs which crippled him and caused financial hardship to his family. Saleh is still looking for a job.*

A Child Prisoner Goes on Hunger Strike

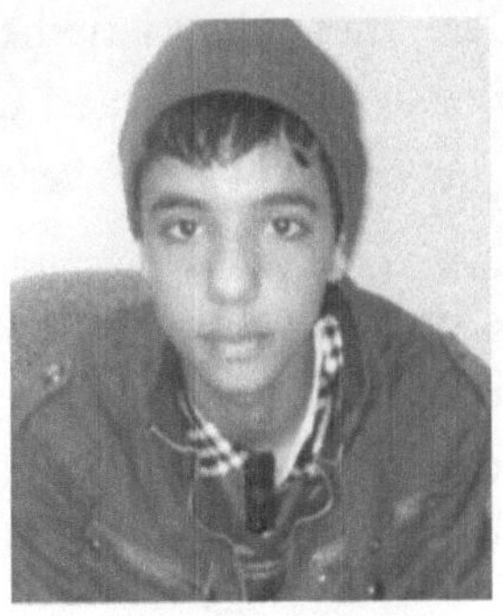

Osama Soboh
Age 14
Jenin

IT was a few days before the summer holidays. I had been really looking forward to the holidays after a tough year of homework and exams.

It was a lovely summer day and I had just finished one of my final exams. I went to a park in our village with my friends, relieved that the pressure of studies had lifted.

However a nightmare was about to happen. A Zionist military vehicle was waiting for us near one of the main roads. As it drove towards us, we ran away. We thought that we had got away, but the soldiers kept following us until they captured me and my friend. They started checking our names and features with names and pictures they had. I hadn't expected this level of hatred. But then I experienced something far worse that I had never imagined.

Soldiers with grumpy faces and huge bodies surrounded us. They stripped us and placed us against the wall of one of the military vehicles. Then, they left their racist marks on our bodies as they beat and humiliated us. We experienced so much sorrow. Our pleas for help were only answered by echoes.

Although I was only 13, and I suffered such inhumane treatment, I held onto my dignity, a key part of my identity. I refused to confess after the interrogator showed me a photo of me throwing stones at Aljalamieh military checkpoint. I was sent to solitary confinement, as punishment, where I lived in what seemed like a graveyard.

To make time pass quicker, I thought of tiny details which I had experienced in my lifetime. I was in a narrow cell with no window or regular light, apart from some light which flashed on and off in a disturbing manner. It was used as a form of punishment and psychological torture against me. I marked mornings and evenings by the timing of food portions given to me. Although they knew I suffered from Asthma, they kept the air-conditioning on the whole time. My health deteriorated as a result and led to a dangerous episode one night. I started to sweat and breathe quickly. I felt like I was suffocating. I yelled at the jailors who did not answer me. I felt dizzy and then fell to the ground. I felt like I was dying. They finally answered my calls, but I would never forget that night. That night planted in my heart the hatred of injustice for the rest of my life.

After all those disturbing incidents and pain, which weakened my small body, I decided to protest, using my own way. What could a prisoner do to protest against humiliation except by refusing food? I went on a hunger strike for one week, in which I only had water and salt. Dignity refused to leave my Palestinian body.

I suffered a lot during my imprisonment which lasted for several months. When I was at court I longed to see my family, to chat with them and touch their hands. But soldiers stood between us like a concrete wall preventing us from speaking to each other and even using sign language. They were very tough times, but my spirit is still high and my body is still strong. ♦

---

* *Osama did not complete his studies and left school after his release when he was in ninth grade. His family started a small shop for him to help him make a living. He is in good health and gets along with his family.*

Prison Gave Me a Headache

Saed Salah
Age 17
Jenin

I SUFFER from terrible headaches which prevent me from moving much or even standing still. Whenever they come on I put my hand on my head and close my eyes. I look around for anything that might ease the pain. I often take a tablet and place my head on a pillow – but the pain never really goes away.

Every time I get a headache, I remember my time in prison, the sorrow and the suffering and in particular the headaches. It was inside that horrid prison, that my headache journey began, with the medication I was given exacerbating it – something I only realised after my release.

One day, I was taking part in a popular protest near our village when Israeli soldiers arrested me. When the first one attacked me, I pushed him away. But he returned, like a monster attacking my small body. Through his thuggish and humiliating acts he revealed to me the hatred inside his heart. He threw me inside a nearby military vehicle, as other soldiers looked on with glee at his humiliation of a 17 year old boy.

My body was screaming out in pain for help. The other boys and I who were arrested were thrown out into the heavy rain. The raindrops felt like bullets hitting our heads on that cold and stormy day. We were still blindfolded and tightly shackled – the scars on my wrist remained for more than one month.

To keep my mind occupied as I passed the time in prison, I used to try and imagine many things and then focus on one scene. I wanted to recall it carefully to keep myself busy and to enable me to travel to a more beautiful world, full of entertainment and smiles.

We were taken to one of the interrogation centres, where we were beaten, threatened and generally terrorised to push us to confess to throwing stones. I was sentenced to four months in prison. It felt like four decades in a cemetery of the living. I never imagined that my name would be part of a prison's records, that I would know the ghost of imprisonment.

They began as short waves of pain, which accelerated and prevented me from functioning. I held my head all day and complained of pain, yet I got no attention.

The headaches were more severe when the weather was extremely cold as I didn't have enough thick clothes and couldn't buy any. I was given some medicines by the jailors, but they made me worse.

Now, although I am free and my condition has improved to some extent, the medicine they gave me still affects me. I became another person. I get angry quickly, which never happened before imprisonment. I don't hate my prison experience, but every time I get a headache, I curse the jailors for what they did to me. ♦

---

* *After his release, Saed left school and never completed his studies. Saed has been seeing a psychologist since he was released from prison as he had become nervous and moody. He has not been able to work due to his health conditions.*

I Met My Brother In Prison

Shadi Al-A'awar
Age 16
Jerusalem

THAT night I couldn't sleep. It's a feeling that anyone might have, especially those suspecting that something bad might happen. People call this intuition, but in Jerusalem, we live it each and every day.

That night I thought about everything. My friends, my imprisoned brother and my family until eventually I fell asleep. I didn't know why it was so hard to sleep until I heard the sounds of monsters on our roof. I woke up to check that what I heard was real. Soldiers attacked from every direction. They searched our house and forced us into one room. I had a feeling that they were looking for me. I was right.

After double-checking my name and my features, the soldiers took me to one of their vehicles. I was heavily beaten and later transferred to Almaskoybia interrogation centre. My mind was racing, thinking about imprisonment and how tough it would be, drawing on the stories that my brother had told me. I was almost instantly homesick, as if I had been taken for a year away from my family.

The soldiers subjected me to long hours of interrogation to force me to confess that I was involved in throwing stones. They claimed to act as humans, but once the person asking the questions left the interrogation room, they would subject me to the most brutal forms of torture. I will never forget those moments that felt like I was about to die.

Later, I was transferred to a prison near Tel Aviv. I never expected that brutality would be the norm. I thought mercy would still have a place in their hearts. They are humans after all. I discovered otherwise when I was placed into the prison with criminal Zionist prisoners who were drug addicts. I was sure that they did that, to allow for lawlessness to prevail and for those criminals to assault and humiliate me.

At every stage of my imprisonment, the picture of my imprisoned brother would not leave me. It was as if I was praying to God to allow me to meet him. One day, I was transferred to Al-Ramleh prison. There, I saw many shackled prisoners, just like me. I was searching their faces. My heart told me that amongst them was my brother who I missed the most. Suddenly, I heard someone calling my name. I looked around and saw my brother. I thought I was dreaming. A smile came over my face for the first time since I had been captured. I felt I was in a familiar place and I no longer cared about being imprisoned.

My brother and I were transferred to Ofik prison. We exchanged stories, memories and dreams of going back to our home one day. We chatted about everything – the walls of our home, our small room and scattered books and how we used to fight about everything. We talked about our passionate mother and my father who works very hard for us to survive and our friends in the neighbourhood. We both laughed for the first time since we had been imprisoned. These beautiful moments were regularly interrupted by soldiers who stormed our cell. They assaulted my brother as I stood powerless, unable to do anything to help him. The scene was extremely tough on me. I wished I was in his shoes so that he could be fine. After several attacks, my brother was taken to solitary confinement for about 17 days.

Apparently everyone wants to return home from prison. This was not the case for me. I would have preferred to have stayed in prison rather than being put under house arrest for four months. Every night whilst at home, I would taste a different sadness and every day, I would close my eyes for hours trying to draw a more beautiful picture of tomorrow.

♦

Childhood Filled with Fear

Yousef Al-Rishq
Age 13
Jerusalem

Every time I remember that day, my body shivers and my senses awake. Not out of fear, but out of hatred for an Occupation that has deprived me of my rights as a child.

I love remembering the tiniest details of my simple and peaceful life, especially my family. But the day I was seized from my family is engrained forever in my memory.

It was 4 in the morning when we were woken up by the sound of Israeli soldiers banging on our door. Without waiting for us to answer, they smashed their way in and turned the whole place into a complete mess. My family didn't know why they'd come to our house until one of them mentioned my name. I was surprised, but my father was completely shocked. I was just 13. The soldiers claimed that I had been summoned to appear at court, but my father refused to let them take me. After a heated row, they accepted that my father could bring me later that morning for interrogation – at 9am.

Unsurprisingly, I could not go back to sleep. I thought a lot and felt sad and full of pain. My dad looked extremely worried and my mother was in distress trying to wipe her tears before they rolled down her cheeks. Those few hours felt like forever.

I went to the interrogation centre with my father. At first, they refused to allow him to be present during questioning, but he insisted. They finally allowed him to be there, but strictly under the condition that he did not say a word during the interrogation. And so it began. They threatened me and I was worried that they might beat me. My father sneezed and they ordered him out of the room. He tried to come back inside, but they didn't allow him to return. Instead they placed him under house arrest for a week!

I was interrogated for nine hours, which was horrendous. But they did eventually let me go. I returned home and my mother hugged me, then took me to my room holding my hand as if she was worried something else might happen to me. That day was so long. I am in such pain recalling it. The horror of interrogation, the sadness and fear are planted in me and will never leave.

At home, they threatened me with arrest and fines if I spoke to my friends or used any electronic means of communication. If I was ill, I had to call them to get permission to leave the house to go to the hospital. I wish

I could erase those horrific memories, as fear still controls me and my family. Will I ever be able to return to my life, school and friends again, without the fear of having my childhood further violated by the Occupation and its 'laws'? ♦

Arrested On My Birthday

Zuhair Al-Ahmad
Age 17
Jenin

I WOKE up early. I looked in the mirror and saw a young and shiny face. "Happy birthday" I whispered to myself. It was my 17th birthday. 17 years with my parents, for whom I was their only son. I receive a great amount of love and appreciation from them. I am not a spoiled kid though and I am not shy or cowardly.

That same day, there was to be a protest in solidarity with Palestinian hunger-striker Samer Issawi, the hero of "empty stomachs' battle". I did not hesitate to participate. I felt proud and strong from inside because people like Samer will lead us to live a dignified life. I took part in the protest which turned into clashes with the Occupation soldiers. I threw stones at them fearless of the possibility of capture. Once the clashes had become less intense I looked at my watch and thought of going back to my family's home. Suddenly though, out of nowhere, I heard the engine of a huge vehicle. People near me shouted at me to run away. At that moment I wanted and perhaps needed to challenge that vehicle and its roaring engines.

The sound came closer and closer. The vehicle hit my small body sending me flying. I fell a few metres away and I really thought I was dead. But the voices of soldiers who were beating me reminded me that I was still alive.

They hit me with the backs of their guns as if I was a grown man. My body was weak. They carried me to their military vehicle where I was continually beaten for another 30 minutes.

One of my fingers was broken. I knew it was broken because I was in excruciating pain. I screamed for help, but there was no one to help me. They beat me even more and their brutality increased. I felt like I was going to faint.

I was transferred to Aljalamieh military checkpoint with a number of other child prisoners. We were thrown out of the vehicles into the heavy rain and we were left to the cold weather to further torment our bodies. We screamed of pain, but again, not one person came to our rescue. We had no food or drink for hours and hours. Then, we were taken for interrogation. Despite the pain I was in, I refused to confess to throwing stones at the soldiers. After the end of the interrogation, we were given rotten food, but I was so hungry that I ate it.

I was transferred to prison where more chapters of suffering began, which I had never anticipated. I kept thinking how that day would have ended if I had not been arrested. Had my parents made a birthday cake for me? Would they have given me some presents? I wanted to hug them and kiss their hands.

In prison I missed the sun. Everything was painful in prison, even my attempts to get rid of pain caused more pain, like when they removed my bad teeth without any analgesia. I didn't have even one peaceful night in the prison. When I eventually left the prison, I looked at the sun happily. I felt dizzy. Prison is dark, but prisoners have so much light in their hearts, that can never fade away. ♦

---

* *Zuhair left school upon his release. He enrolled in a training course to become a tiler so that he can help his family financially. In spite of all he has experienced, his psychological well-being is excellent.*

12-year-old Dima al-Wawi, believed to be the youngest female Palestinian to be incarcerated by Israel, was released to her family on 24 April, 2016, after she spent two-and-a-half months in Israeli prison for an alleged attempted manslaughter carried out at an illegal Israeli settlement.

Dima's Eyes – A Poem

By Aida Qasim

Eyes like an unfinished poem possess my spirit
They rise the moon out of its slothiness
Shaking away the stillness of my pillow
I shudder and solicit a memory:
Sweet mint tea in my aunt's patio on
Salaheddein Street in Al Quds
Long oblong sesame Ka'ek warm as the freshly boiled
salt of the earth Nabulsi cheese melts
in my mouth
Be still eyes old as Canaan

But
Can't you see I have not slept in a thousand years?
Oh, the molasses night clings onto me like
a hungry stray cat
Go play hide and seek in the crevasses of hills
with your friends
I close my eyes again to pull back the black shroud
molesting the glassy blue sky
And beckon the morning to fill my head
with chatter
Be still eyes old as Canaan

But
Can't you see the battalion riding my slight
shoulders?
The storekeepers open their shops before athan
in the old city
Put on your school uniform and tie a pretty
white ribbon in your hair
Be still eyes old as Canaan

But
My childhood is wilting before you like
Gazan carnations
The neighbors swarm around my bed as they did the
summer I turned nine and caught the mumps
An irate rooster rouses a farmer from his slumber
Sing like the swallow of the Galilee
Be still eyes old as Canaan

But
I have sacrificed my beautiful long hair for
a loaf of bread
So that the blessings of Ya'qoub's well
can heal the wounds of my people

Mwazi figs slide between my fingers at
the retreat of August
A sage dawn descends upon the room
Be still eyes old as Canaan
Halawani grapes still hang in your vine waiting
to be plucked

---

* *Aida Qasim teaches Psychology and Social Work and is also completing her Doctorate in Social Work. She contributed this poem to PalestineChronicle.com.*

The Hares Boys

The car accident

At around 18:30 on Thursday 14 March 2013, a car crashed into the back of a truck on Road 5 in Salfit Governorate, occupied Palestine. The driver and her 3 daughters were injured, one of them – seriously. The driver, Adva Biton, was going back to the illegal Israeli settler colony of Yakir when the accident occurred. She later claimed the accident was due to Palestinian youth throwing stones at her car. The driver of the truck, having testified immediately after the accident that he had pulled over because of a flat tyre, later changed his mind and said he had seen stones by the road.

There were no witnesses to the car accident. Nobody had seen any children or youth throwing stones that day.

The arrests

In the early hours of Friday 15 March 2013, masked Israeli soldiers, some with attack dogs, stormed the village of Hares, which is close to Road 5. More than 50 soldiers broke the doors of the villagers' houses, demanding the whereabouts of their teenage sons. Ten boys were arrested that night, blindfolded, handcuffed, and transferred to an unknown location. The families were not informed of their sons' alleged wrongdoings.

Two days later, a second wave of violent arrests took place. At around 3 o'clock in the morning, the Israeli army, accompanied by the Shabak (the Israeli secret service), entered the homes of 3 Palestinian adolescents. They had a piece of paper with their names in Hebrew. After forcing all the family members into one room, taking away their phones so that they wouldn't call for help, and interrogating them, the soldiers handcuffed their sons, all aged 16-17.

"Kiss and hug your mother goodbye," a Shabak agent told one boy. *"You may never see her again."*

A week later, Israeli army jeeps again entered the village and arrested several boys, who had just come back home from school. The soldiers lined all of them up, including a 6-year-old, and threatened at gunpoint their uncle who pleaded for the soldiers to at least release the youngest children. The army then randomly chose 3 boys, handcuffed them behind their backs, blindfolded them, and took them away. The families were not informed about either the allegations against their children, or their exact location.

In total, 19 boys from the neighbouring villages of Hares and Kifl Hares were arrested in relation to the settler car accident. None of them had previously had any history of stone-throwing. After violent interrogations, most of the minors were released, except for five, who remain in Megiddo, an Israeli adult prison.

These are the Hares Boys.

30 January 2016

The Five Hares Boys to Spend 15 Years in Prison for a Crime that Never Happened

Press Release – 30 January 2016
by Free The Hares Boys campaign

THURSDAY 28 January, 2016 was the day when the five youth known internationally as the Hares Boys were officially sentenced to 15 years' imprisonment in an Israeli occupation prison, by an Israeli occupation military court, in a land occupied by Israel.

The sentence was announced following almost three years of uncertainty since Mohammed Suleiman, Mohammed Kleib, Ali Shamlawi, Tamer Souf and Ammar Souf – residents of Hares village in the West Bank of Palestine – were arrested and accused of 'attempted murder' by stone-throwing after an illegal Israeli settler car crashed into a truck parked on a road next to their village. That was mid-March 2013, light years away when you are 16 years old and locked up in an occupation dungeon for a car accident you had nothing to do with; a crime that never happened.

Thursday's sentencing was a plea deal offered by the Israeli military prosecutor that involved 'fines' of 30,000 NIS (appr. €7,100 or $7,750) per boy to be paid to the settler driver as

Protestors outside the Labour party conference in Brighton urging the Labour Party to drop G4S from providing the security for its conferences. Later, in November 2015, the Labour Party announced that it would no longer be using G4S for its conference security.

'compensation'. One of her daughters died two years after the crash from pneumonia complications attributed to neurological damage experienced during the accident. Failure to accept the deal, it was implied, would result in extended prison sentences. The boys' families felt they had no choice but to accept. *"We took the bad to avoid the worst,"* they said in their despair.

Almost three years of legal battles in military courts that have a record of convicting Palestinians at a rate very close to 100%.

Almost three years of military court 'hearings' that last just a few minutes, conducted by Israeli military personnel in Hebrew, a language neither the boys nor their families understand; the soldier-translator would rarely do their job properly and would instead prefer to play with their phone.

Almost three years of dozens – well over 100 – such 'hearings' in metal cages that pass for a House of Justice, only to find out that your incarceration is prolonged once again.

Almost three years knowing that you 'confessed', under torture, of throwing stones at settler cars, that you 'confessed' after being beaten up and psychologically intimidated, and spending days in solitary confinement without access to a lawyer, and that this 'confession' is the only 'evidence' the military tribunal has against you, yet that it would probably be enough for them to convict you.

Almost three years of mothers, fathers, sisters, and brothers not knowing whether you would be home for the next

The mother of Ali Shamlawi addresses Members of the House of Commons and House of Lords in the UK Parliament.

Ramadan or to finish your high school exams. Not knowing when they could finally hug you and talk to you without a broken telephone through a dirty glass window.

Almost three years of international efforts to bring the case of the Hares Boys to the eyes and consciences of those in power, and to demand justice. We invited you to protest, organize demonstrations, write to your MPs, write to your embassy in Tel Aviv, attend military court 'hearings', collect money to help the families deal with the financial burden, to spread the message about the injustice being committed to these young lives of Palestine. And you responded, in your hundreds and in your thousands, from Costa Rica to France, from Mexico to Britain. We thank you for that. You've been a lifeline of support to the boys' families in such devastating time.

But the fight is not over.

If we stop demanding justice, five young men are to spend the next 15 years of their lives in prison. For them and other prisoners, their families, communities and their people, we must continue the struggle.

We invite you all, wherever you are, to join hands with us, to strengthen the efforts to achieve justice and FREEDOM for the five youth of Hares, Palestine. ♦

Website: https://haresboys.wordpress.com/
Facebook: https://www.facebook.com/FreeTheHaresBoys/

The following affidavits were taken by
Defence for Children International-Palestine
several weeks after the boys were
arrested and interrogated.

Some grammatical and spelling errors have been corrected.

Name of victim	'Ammar Abed Nayef Sof
Date of birth	27 September 1997
Date of arrest	17 March 2013
Age at time of arrest	16 years
Accusation	Throwing stones
Place of residence	Haris, Salfit
Date affidavit was taken	17 April 2013

*After having been warned to tell the truth and nothing but the truth or else I shall be subjected to penal action, I the undersigned, **'Ammar Abed Nayef Sof**, holder of ID No. ********, a resident of Haris, Salfit, would like to declare the following:*

1. I am from the village of Haris, Salfit. I do not know when I was born exactly, but I am 16 and a half years old. I finished the eighth grade and dropped out. I was arrested on 17 March 2013. My family consists of 11

members, and my father sells bottled gas. Our financial conditions are of average.

2. On 17 March 2013, at around 3:30 a.m., I woke up to banging on the door. I was sleeping in the room with my seven-year old brother Mohammad, nine-year old brother Moath and eight-year old sister Ayat. My mother went to open the door and asked me to hide and not to get out, because we knew Israeli occupation forces were coming to arrest me because my friends including Mohammad Suleiman were arrested two days ago.

3. My mother opened the door and I heard soldiers storming the house, and my little siblings started crying and screaming, so I had to get out. I got out and went to the living room where I saw many soldiers. An intelligence officer asked me for my name and I answered him. He introduced himself as Captain Shukri, the Israeli intelligence officer in charge of our area.

4. Shukri said he had come to arrest me. *"Do you know why?"* he asked me and I told him no. *"Yes, you do. It's because you threw stones on 14 March. Your friends told us this and we're going to arrest you right now,"* Shukri said. Two soldiers grabbed me and dragged me out of the house and did not allow me to say goodbye to my family. They tied my hands behind my back with a single plastic cord and blindfolded me. I could not see anything.

5. After that, soldiers grabbed me and started running really fast on a rough road. They made me walk for about 300 metres. They were slapping me and kicking

me. They knocked me down three times. Then they stopped me near a military jeep and one of them pushed me hard inside the jeep and I fell on the ground. While I was lying on the ground, they started beating me hard and one of them hit me all over my body with the stock of his rifle.

6. After that, one of the soldiers pulled me up and threw me into the military jeep. They made me sit on the metal floor. I felt I was sitting on someone's feet. When I arrived at the settlement of Yaqir, I found out I was sitting on Tamer's feet who was arrested that night. Tamer Sof is from my village.

7. The jeep started travelling and soldiers did not tell me where they were taking me. They slapped me and Tamer and shouted at us in Hebrew without stopping. The jeep arrived at the settlement of Yaqir near my village. Soldiers pulled me out with Tamer and made us sit on the ground and beat us from time to time. They did not allow us to use the bathroom.

8. Soldiers took me to a room, where they removed the blindfold and kept my hands tied. A military doctor asked me a few questions about my health but did not examine me physically. I remember seeing Tamer when they removed my blindfold. His mouth and nose were bleeding. At around 3:00 p.m., soldiers transferred Tamer to Al Jalame interrogation and detention centre, but they kept me sitting on the ground until around 6:00 p.m. They mistreated me and kept beating me. They did not allow me to use the bathroom at all.

9.   At around 6:00 p.m., soldiers from Nihshon unit arrived at the settlement, untied me and removed the blindfold. They handcuffed my hands from front and shackled my feet. They put me in their car and transferred me to Al Jalame centre. I arrived at around 8:00 p.m., and a jailer from Israel Prison Service took me to a room and strip searched me. He gave me prison clothes and took me to an interrogation room.

10. I entered the interrogation room and there was a Jewish interrogator who spoke fluent Arabic. He said his name is Mimi. He made me sit in a metal chair in the middle of the room and tied my hands and feet to it. The chair was few inches above the floor and it was really painful to sit in it. He started interrogating me without informing me of my rights, including my right to remain silent. Also, he interrogated me alone without the presence of a lawyer or a family member.

11. *"You're accused of throwing stones on 14 March with your friends from a hill on the main street and hitting an Israeli car,"* he said. *"Denying it won't do you any good because your friends already confessed to everything,"* he added. He read to me detailed statements but I am not sure whether they were true or fake. I however decided to confess so I would suffer no more, so I confessed to throwing stones.

12. He interrogated me for three hours. He interrogated me three times in the same manner. That day and after interrogation had ended, a jailer took me to cell 10 and kept me detained there in solitary confinement for four days.

13. The cell was very small and there was a mattress thrown on the floor. The walls had rough surface and I could not lean against them. The lights were dim yellow and you cannot look at them. There were no windows, and the smell that was coming from the toilet was unbearable. I could not tell day from night.

14. I was detained in Al Jalame centre for 19 days, four of which in solitary confinement and the rest with Tamer. On 4 April, I was transferred to Megiddo prison. When I arrived, a jailer from Israel Prison Service strip searched me and detained me in the juvenile section number three, where I am currently held in the same room with children my age.

15. After three days of my arrest, I appeared before a judge for the first time in Al Jalame centre where my detention was extended twice, but I do not remember the exact days. On 9 April, I appeared in Salem military court and my detention was extended for six days. On 14 April, my detention was extended for five days until 18 April.

Signed by:
’Ammar Abed Nayef Sof
17 April 2013

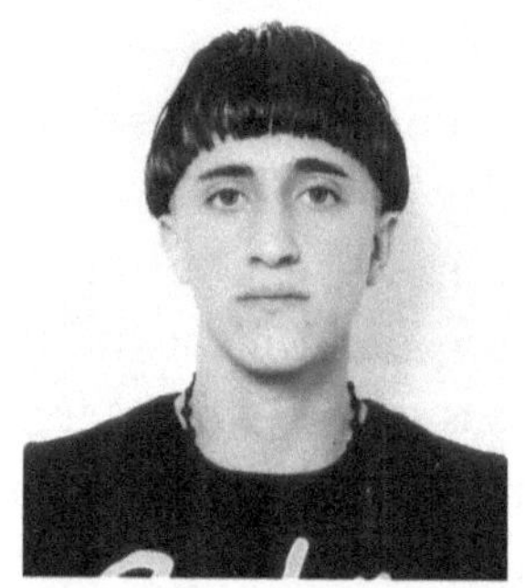

Name of victim	Ali Yasin Ali Shamlawi
Date of birth	12 January 1997
Date of arrest	17 March 2013
Age at time of arrest	16 years
Accusation	Throwing stones
Place of residence	Haris, Salfit
Date affidavit was taken	10 April 2013

*After having been warned to tell the truth and nothing but the truth or else I shall be subjected to penal action, I the undersigned, **Ali Yasin Ali Shamlawi**, holder of ID No. ********, a resident of Haris, Salfit, would like to declare the following:*

1. I am from the village of Haris, Salfit. I was born on 12 January 1997. I am in the 11th grade. I was arrested on 17 March 2013. My family consists of eight members,

and my father is unemployed. The family's financial conditions are very bad.

2. On 17 March 2013, at around 3:00 a.m., I woke up to banging on our door. I got up and went out to the living room and found all my family there. My father opened the door and around 15 Israeli soldiers stormed the living room and surrounded from all directions. They just kept looking at us for about 15 minutes without saying a word.

3. Then, two intelligence officers came in. One of them introduced himself as Captain Shukri, the intelligence officer in charge of our village. The other one was Inviko. Shukri said he wanted to ask each one of us a few questions. He took my father to the kitchen and came back a few minutes later and took my brother, Hakim (23).

4. Then, he took me to the kitchen and asked me for my date of birth, my name and mobile phone number. I told him I did not have a mobile phone, but he called me a liar and went out to the living room and asked my father loudly whether I had one or not. My father asked him to look in the drawer in the kitchen. Shukri looked at me and called me a liar.

5. I got up and wanted to give him my mobile phone, but he refused. He grabbed me by my arm and asked me to sit tight and don't move. He asked my brother to fetch it, and my brother did so, and Shukri took it and gave it to one of the soldiers. *"We're taking you with us because you've been causing a lot of trouble,"* Shukri said to me

and I told him I did not do anything. *"Then, you'll come home,"* he said. He did not tell me why exactly they were taking me.

6. After that, a soldier grabbed me hard by my hand and took me out of the house. He made me stand against the wall and searched me. Then, he tied my hands behind my back with a single plastic cord that he tightened really hard and blindfolded me. Then, they put me inside a military jeep that was near the house and made me sit on the metal floor.

7. There were other soldiers inside the jeep. They started beating me really hard for no reason. They were kicking me and hitting me on the head. I was an easy target. I mean I was sitting on the metal floor in front of them, and they were sitting on seats surrounding me from all directions. They kept beating me for like half an hour, during which time the jeep arrived at Yaqir military camp near my village. They did not tell me where they were taking me.

8. Soldiers pulled me out of the jeep and took me to a room, where they untied me and removed my blindfold. A doctor examined me and asked me general questions about my health. Then, they re-tied and re-blindfolded me and took me to another room, where they made me sit on the floor and would beat me from time to time. They did not allow me to use the bathroom. They did not bring me food or water either.

9. At around 6:30 a.m., they took me out of the room and untied me and removed the blindfold. Three soldiers from Nihshon unit, which is a unit affiliated with Israel

Prison Service had arrived. They took me back to the room and ordered me to take all my clothes off to search me, as they claimed. I took them off and stood there completely naked. Then, they gave me my clothes back and I put them on quickly.

10. After that, they handcuffed my hands from front, and my feet as well. They put me in their vehicle and transferred me to Al Jalame interrogation and detention centre. I arrived at around 9:30 a.m., and a jailer took me straightaway to a room and strip searched me, before detaining me in a small bathroom for about half an hour.

11. After that, he detained me in cell 36, which is a small cell for one person. There was a mattress on the floor and it smelled horribly. There was a toilet and nasty smell was coming out from it. There were no windows; just two gaps to let air in and out. The lights were yellow and were on the entire time, and that can be harmful to the eyes. The walls were gray and I could not lean against them because they had a rough surface.

12. I did not know day from night. I was brought food through a hole in the door. That day I spent about half an hour in the cell. Then, the jailer came back and took me to interrogation on the second floor, because he made me climb up stairs. He took me to an interrogation room, where a Jewish interrogator named Steve was sitting behind a desk with a computer in front of him. He spoke fluent Arabic.

13. There was a metal chair a few inches above the floor in the middle of the room. The interrogator made me

sit there and tied my hands and feet to the chair. He did this to me every time he interrogated me and for hours.

14. That day, he started interrogating me without explaining my rights, such as my right to remain silent. I did not have a lawyer or a family member present. The same thing applies to the rest of the interrogations rounds.

15. He accused me of throwing stones and I denied it, but he called me a liar. *"All your friends who got arrested before you did said in their statements that you threw stones with them,"* he said and sat behind the desk and started typing on the computer. Another interrogator came in and said to me, *'Seems you're choosing the hard way, but its better you confess for your own good.'*

16. *"Come with me to see your friends confessing in front of you,"* the second interrogator said. *"I don't want to go with you,"* I said to him. *"What? Are you afraid of the truth?"* he said. He untied me, grabbed me hard by my hand and took me out of the room. He made me stand by a closed door and ordered me to look through the peephole.

17. I looked through the peephole and saw my friend, Mohammad Klaib, who was arrested three days earlier. The interrogator said that Mohammad had confessed. Mohammad could not see me. *"Tell me your confessions in detail,"* the interrogator said to Mohammad, and Mohammad said he threw stones at Israeli cars a day before he got arrested. *"So what do you think now?"* the interrogator said to me.

18. *"He didn't say anything about me,"* I said to the interrogator and he asked Mohammad again. *"What's the name of the boy who threw stones with you? Ali what?"* the interrogator said. *"Ali Shamlawi,"* Mohammad said. He did not see me. He did not know I was standing there behind the door.

19. The interrogator took me back to the interrogation room. *"They all confessed against you, so its better you do it yourself,"* he said. *"They're all lying,"* I said and he dragged me to the window and said, 'Do you see the sun? I'll make you rot in jail and you'll never see it again.' He made me sit in the metal chair and tied me to it. He asked me to confess but I refused.

20. *"Then I'll give my orders to soldiers at checkpoint to cause trouble to your family members because their son is a terrorist,"* he said and asked me where I was on 14 March 2013. I told him I was in school but he called me a liar. *"Do you want to see pictures of you on the mountain throwing stones at Israeli cars?"* he said and I told I did not want to see any pictures. He did not show me any pictures.

21. I told him that on Thursday, 14 March, I came home from school and had lunch with my family. Then, I sat with my cousin Taiseer until around afternoon prayer, when I went to play football in the school yard. Then, I came home and heard ambulances and was told there had been a car accident in the main street.

22. The interrogator stopped me there and called me a liar. *"If you don't tell me you were throwing stones with your friends, I'll bring your mother down here and torture her in*

front of you," he shouted. *"Do whatever you want,"* I said to him. *"You have no honour. You don't care about your mother?"* he said.

23. He interrogated me for hours. At around 6:00 p.m., he took me to a cell downstairs. He opened the door and I saw Tamer Sof. *"Is it true that you threw stones with Ali, Tamer, Ammar, Mohammad Jum'aa and Mohammad Mahdi?"* the interrogator asked Tamer and Tamer said yes. The interrogator took me back to the interrogation room. *"It's true I was with them, but I didn't throw any stones,"* I said to him and he got really angry.

24. He started screaming and pulling my hair. *"They'll get reduced sentences, but you'll get a much higher one for lying,"* he shouted and that scared me a lot, so I told him I threw two stones only but they did not hit anyone. He wrote down my statement and I signed it. I was then taken back to the cell and I slept for the first time since I was arrested.

25. I spent five days in solitary confinement from 17 until 22 March, and I was not allowed to see a lawyer. I would like to say that I was interrogated only once by the intelligence; the one I already mentioned. It lasted for a long time. At the end, the police took my statement, in which I confessed to throwing stones on 14 March, and about one and a half years ago with Mohammad Sof. I had to confess, but I never threw any stones.

26. I was detained in Al Jalame centre for 19 days from 17 March until 4 April. I spent five days in solitary confinement. I spent about one hour in cell 36. After the first round of interrogation, I was detained in cell 23

for 14 days. I spent the rest of the days in cell 20. All the cells are the same.

27. On 4 April, I was transferred to Megiddo prison. When I got here, a jailer strip searched me and detained me in the juvenile section number three, where I am currently detained with children my age.

28. During my detention in Al Jalame centre, my detention was extended three times in Al Jalame military court, and once in Salem military court which was yesterday; 9 April, until 14 April.

Signed by:
Ali Yasin Ali Shamlawi
10 April 2013

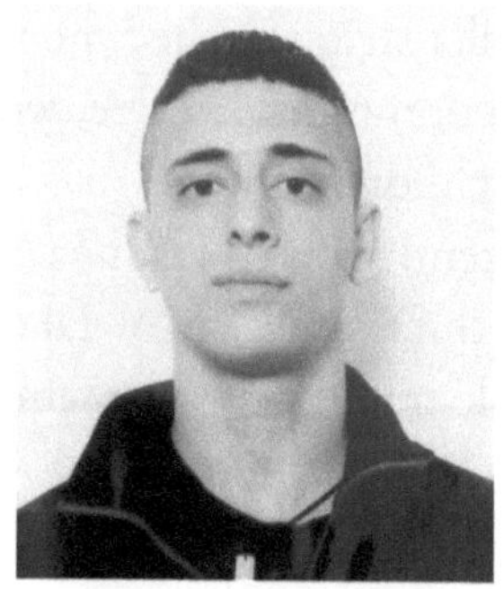

Name of victim	Mohammad Jum'aa Mohammad Klaib
Date of birth	20 June 1996
Date of arrest	15 March 2013
Age at time of arrest	16 years
Accusation	Throwing stones
Place of residence	Haris, Salfit
Date affidavit was taken	10 April 2013

After having been warned to tell the truth and nothing but the truth or else I shall be subjected to penal action, I the undersigned, **Mohammad Jum'aa Mohammad Klaib**, *holder of ID No. ********, a resident of Haris, Salfit, would like to declare the following:*

1. I am from the village of Haris, Salfit. I was born on 20 June 1996. I am in the 11th grade. I was arrested on 15

March 2013. My family consists of 14 members, as my father is married to two. He is a labourer. The family's financial conditions are not good.

2. On 15 March 2013, at around 5:00 a.m., my mother came to the room where I was sleeping with my brothers Rifa't (7) and Abboud (14) and told me there were soldiers knocking on our door and apparently they had come to arrest one of you. I was on the second floor, and soldiers were knocking on the front door downstairs.

3. My father opened the door and came upstairs to tell me that soldiers wanted me and my brother Nizar (19). I came downstairs with my brother, and a soldier asked me for my name and I told him. He checked my ID and told me I was under arrest without telling me why. *"We'll take you to interrogation and you should be polite,"* he said. *"I'll be polite if you don't harm my family,"* I said to him.

4. A soldier grabbed me hard by my hands and took me out of the house. They made me walk all the way to the centre of the village near the mosque about 50 metres away. One of them then tied my hands behind my back with a single plastic cord that he tightened so much I still have marks around my wrists.

5. Soldiers made me walk to the school about one kilometre away. They made me stand against the wall of the school where they took pictures of me alone and with them with their mobile phone cameras. One of them insulted me; *'Your mother's a c**t, m**********r.'* I recall one of them was really tall and took a lot of pictures of me.

6. Then, soldiers brought a dog and unleashed him and I was really scared. The dog was so close to attack me, but one of them grabbed him and tied him. He would make him approach me really close to scare me. About 15 minutes later, they brought Mahmoud and made him stand against the wall next to me. Mahmoud was released one week later.

7. After that, soldiers blindfolded me and made me walk with Mahmoud to the observation tower at the entrance of the village about three kilometers away. When we got there, a soldier lifted me and threw me hard on a pile of gravel. He then kicked me with his military boots while I was still lying on the ground. My legs swelled and they still hurt me.

8. At around 6:30 a.m., soldiers put me in a military truck and made me sit on the floor. There were other children inside the truck, including Rabe'a Dawood, Ahmad Fayeq and Osama (I don't know his last name). They were released a few days later. The truck arrived at a military camp but I do not know its name.

9. Soldiers pulled us all out of the truck and made us sit on the ground. One of them approached me and tied my legs with a rope he found on the ground. I saw him from under the blindfold. He also untied my hands and tied them again behind my back with two plastic cords next to each other. The cords were very tight and hurt me.

10. After that, I was taken to a military clinic where soldiers untied me but kept me blindfolded. A doctor checked my pressure and asked me general questions

about my health, with my eyes still blindfolded. Then, a soldier retied me behind my back with two plastic cords that he tightened very much. They took me out and made me sit on the ground until around afternoon prayer, with giving me any food or water and without allowing me to use the bathroom. There were dogs around me as well.

11. As I was hearing a muezzin leading calls to afternoon prayer, soldiers untied me and removed the blindfold. Soldiers from Nihshon unit arrived and took me to a room where they strip searched me after ordering me to take all my clothes off. I was completely naked. Then, they handcuffed my hands from front. They also shackled my feet. They put me in their car and transferred me to Al Jalame interrogation and detention centre. I was alone in the car without the rest of the children.

12. I arrived at Al Jalame centre about two hours later, and a jailer took me to a room where he strip searched me and gave me prison clothes before detaining me in cell 26 for about half an hour. The cell was so small it barely fit one person. A mattress was on the floor and there was a toilet. The lights were yellow and the walls were gray with rough surface, which makes it painful to lean against them. There were no windows, just two gaps to let air in and out. The air that was coming in was really cold and you cannot sleep.

13. About half an hour later, a jailer took me out and made me climb up stairs leading to interrogation rooms. He took me to one of the rooms where I saw a Jewish interrogator who spoke fluent Arabic. The interrogator

made me sit in a low metal chair in the middle of the room and in front of the desk where he was sitting.

14. The interrogator tied my hands and feet to the chair and slapped me hard and ordered me to confess. *"Confess to what?"* I asked. *"Tell me what you did. You have to tell me,"* he said and I told him I did not do anything and that I cannot confess to something I did not do. He did not accuse me of anything.

15. *"You either confess the easy way or the hard way,"* he screamed in my face. *"I don't know what you're talking about. I won't confess to something I didn't do,"* I replied, but he shouted at me and spat on me. He called the jailer in and asked me to *'Take him back to the cell until he rots there.'*

16. I was interrogated for about one hour. The interrogator did not explain my rights like my right to remain silent. He interrogated me without the presence of a lawyer or a family member. As I said earlier, he did not accuse me of anything. He wanted me to confess on my own. He never explained my rights in all the interrogations rounds, and he interrogated me without the presence of a lawyer or a family member.

17. I was taken back to the cell. They did not bring me any food. I had not had any food since they arrested me from home. I asked them to bring me food the following morning but they refused. I asked them for a cigarette and they refused. I was detained in the cell until the following day at around 12:00 p.m., when the jailer took me to the interrogation room.

18. The same interrogator tied me to the metal chair, and I asked him to bring me some food before interrogation because I was very hungry. *"Confess now and I'll bring you food. But if you don't, I don't really mind starving you to death,"* he said to me. He started interrogating me by screaming at me.

19. *"How was your picnic on the mountain? Did you enjoy eating banana? Were the pictures good?"* he said. He was making fun of me. *"I wasn't on the mountain,"* I said. *"Liar,"* he shouted hard and started punching me and kicking me over and over. *"I'm sure you've heard of the detainee from Hebron who died in prison. I'll kill you like we killed him if you don't confess,"* he said to me.

20. I was really scared of him. He interrogated me more than three hours and this time he accused me of throwing stones with the children who were arrested with me. *"What children are you talking about?"* I asked him. *"You know them well,"* he said and started naming them; Tamer Sof, Ammar Sof, Mohammad Suleiman and Ali Yasin. *"I wasn't with them and I didn't throw any stones,"* I said to him. *"Liar, liar,"* he shouted. *"I have evidence and pictures of you on the mountain throwing stones at Israeli cars,"* he said.

21. After three hours of interrogation, I was taken back to the cell. I asked the jailer to bring me some food as I had not had any for two days, but he screamed at me, pushed me inside and closed the door. About an hour later, he brought a small piece of bread and a boiled egg

which I think was boiled like two days ago. It was cold, but I had to eat it despite its nasty smell.

22. At around 9:00 p.m., the door opened and I saw a huge tall jailer standing behind it. *"Do you want a cigarette?"* he said. He got a cigarette out, ripped it off and threw to on the floor to upset me. *"You're despicable and you're getting nothing from us,"* he said and closed the door.

23. On 19 March, I was taken to the snitches' cell. I did not know that. Mohammad Mahdi Sof from my village was there, along with another child named Omar from 'Azzun, Qalqiliya. Mohammad said he confessed to throwing stones. He did not know he was in the snitches' cell.

24. Mohammad said had told the other detainees in the room everything about the organization, and that they wanted to help us out. *"Tell them everything when they ask,"* he said to me. He said he confessed to throwing stones a year ago and one day before I got arrested. *"You got to tell them everything,"* he said.

25. At first I did not want to tell the snitches anything. Two men, Abu Ahmad and Abu Abed in their forties I think, sat with me and said they were from the organization and I should tell them everything. I told them I threw stones about one and a half years ago with Idrees when soldiers stormed the village and demolished some houses in 12 December 2012.

26. I told the snitches everything. I spent that night with them. The following evening, 20 March, I was taken back to the cell. Shortly after that, I was taken for

interrogation. The same interrogator tied me to the chair and took a piece of paper out of his pocket. He told me everything I had told the men in the other room. That's when I knew they were snitches. It was all written on the paper.

27. When he finished reading the paper, he said I got no choice but to confess. *"You already did it,"* he said. *"It's all lies,"* I said and he shouted at me and called me a liar. He gave me papers in Arabic and ordered me to sign them, but I refused. *"I'll beat you if you don't confess,"* he said and I said to him, *'Beat me as much as you want because I don't care and I'm not signing those papers either.'*

28. He kept shouting at me and threatening me. I was really scared of him, so I confessed to throwing stones about one and a half years ago. Then, he stopped interrogating me and asked the jailer to send me back to the cell. Shortly after that, I knocked on the door of the cell to call the jailer. The door opened and it was the same huge and tall jailer. *"Why did you knock on the door? The next time you do it, I'll come in and f**k you,"* he said and I said to him, *'You can't do anything.'* And he said, *'Wait and see.'*

29. He closed the door and went away, but he came back about five minutes later with two other men. The three of them stormed the cell, and the big one slapped me and kicked me so hard and knocked me down. Then, the three of them started beating me and kept doing it for about 15 minutes, with me screaming from pain.

30. The huge jailer wanted to hit me with a stick, but one of the two men stopped him and said to him, *'Don't get us into trouble.'* They stopped beating me and the huge jailer said to me, *'I'll smash your head if you ever tell anyone about this.'* They went out and kept me on the floor, with my nose bleeding and my face turning into red. I was hurting and feeling so much pain.

31. A jailer came in, picked me off the floor, washed my face, cleaned up the blood and gave me some food. Then, I went to bed. I was kept in the cell for five days without interrogation. Five days later, I was taken back to interrogation. I was in bad shape and hurting, so I decided to confess to everything to get myself out of the cell and put an end to this humiliation. I confessed to throwing stones a day before I got arrested. I was interrogated for a short while and was taken back to the cell.

32. During my detention in Al Jalame centre, I was detained alone in solitary confinement from 15 until 19 March. I spent one night with the snitches. Then, I was taken back to the cell and I spent eight days with Mohammad Sof. I was detained in Al Jalame until 4 April; four days in solitary confinement and the rest with other children.

33. On 4 April, I was transferred to Megiddo prison. When I arrived, a jailer from Israel Prison Service strip searched me and detained me in the juvenile section number three, where I am currently detained with other children my age.

34. I appeared in court for the first time in Al Jalame centre after three days of my detention. My detention was extended three times in Al Jalame. Yesterday, 9 April, I appeared in Salem military court and my detention was extended for the fourth time for six days until 14 April.

Signed by:
Mohammad Jum'aa Mohammad Klaib
10 April 2013

Name of victim	Mohammad Mahdi Saleh Suleiman
Date of birth	10 October 1996
Date of arrest	15 March 2013
Age at time of arrest	16 years
Accusation	Throwing stones
Place of residence	Haris, Salfit
Date affidavit was taken	17 April 2013

After having been warned to tell the truth and nothing but the truth or else I shall be subjected to penal action, I the undersigned, **Mohammad Mahdi Saleh Suleiman**, *holder of ID No. ***********, a resident of Haris, Salfit, would like to declare the following:*

1. I am from the village of Haris, Salfit. I was born on 10 October 1996. I finished the tenth grade and dropped out. I was working in the settlement of Barqan before

I was arrested. My family consists of 12 members. My father has been exiled to Jordan for 15 years by the Israeli intelligence because he was a political activist. He does not work and does not help us at all. As a matter of fact, we are the ones who send him money. My brothers and I work and support the family. Our financial conditions are really harsh. I was arrested on 15 March 2013.

2. On 15 March 2013, at around 3:00 a.m., I woke up to banging on the door. I got up quickly and heard a device that is for opening doors being turned on. But before they could break the door, my brother Odai (21) rushed and opened it. I saw many Israeli soldiers at the door. They asked my brother for his name, and when he told them, one of them pushed him away. I was standing next to him.

3. The soldier asked me for my name and I answered him. When he verified my identity, he dragged me out of the house. Odai had already taken him away and I did not know where they took him, but I was told that he was released later that night.

4. Soldiers took me to the yard outside the house, and one of them pushed me hard against the wall and my back slammed against a metal tap and I felt so much pain and screamed. Three soldiers attacked me straightaway and started punching me. One of them kicked me hard on my legs and knocked me down and the three of them kept kicking me without any mercy for about 15 minutes. I was screaming from the pain.

5. I am sure my family heard me screaming but they did not see anything, because soldiers did not allow them to

come out or open the windows. They kept me lying on the ground for about 15 minutes after beating me hard. Then, they pushed me hard and handcuffed me from front and took me to a military jeep parked about 15 metres from the house.

6. There were three intelligence officers standing near the military jeep. They said their names were Shukri, Steven and Nevek. An Arab officer was with them as well. *"You're under arrest and you should confess during interrogation, but if you don't you'll suffer big time,"* the officer said to me. *"You're wearing sport shoes so you could run fast after throwing stones,"* he said when he saw my Adidas shoes.

7. After that, the Arab officer took me back to the house and made me sit in a chair in the living room. All my family were gathered in one room and were not allowed to come out. The three intelligence officer entered the house as well. Steven, who is a Jewish interrogator but speaks fluent Arabic, approached me and started talking to me.

8. Steven said that the day before, 14 March, stones were thrown at the main street leading to Ari'el settlement and hit an Israeli car. *"You threw stones and we're arresting you because of that. You need to confess during interrogation. It's for your own good unless you want to take the blame for it,"* he said. *"Even so, I'm not confessing to something I didn't do,"* I said to him.

9. Then, soldiers brought four children from my village to the living room. They were Ahmad Fayeq, Osama Musa, Mohammad Hafeth and Mohammad Sedqi. They were

released that night. Soldiers made them stand aside and watch me being beaten hard to intimidate them and make them confess. Soldiers were punching me hard and hitting me on my head. I was screaming from the pain.

10. *"We won't stop until you confess so we won't arrest you. It's better you spare us the time and effort,"* Steven said to me. They kept beating me so hard I felt so much pain and screamed, *'Yes I threw stones.'* I heard my mother screaming and crying in the other room and begging them to stop beating me. My little siblings were crying and screaming too.

11. I was kept inside the house until around 6:30 a.m. They beat me hard, so hard I told Steven that the other four children threw stones as well, even though they did not. I told him later they did not. I had to tell him they threw stones because I was really scared they might keep beating me. Anyway, the children were released later.

12. At around 6:30 a.m., soldiers removed the handcuffs and tied my hands behind my back with a single plastic cord that they tightened so hard it entered into the flesh and left marks for about two weeks. They also blindfolded me and took me out of the house. Two of them grabbed me and made me walk really fast. A third soldier was kicking and hitting me hard on my legs from behind. He hit me hard on my legs with his rifle and knocked me down and they pulled me up.

13. Soldiers made me walk for about 300 metres until we reached a military jeep. They ordered me to get inside but I could not because I could not see anything, so

they pulled me up and threw me inside and I fell on the metal floor. They kept me on the metal floor. When they pulled me up to throw me inside, the blindfold dropped down a little and I managed to see many jeeps parked near the huge metal observation tower near my village.

14. There was an Arab soldier inside the jeep. *"I'll f**k you in the ass, you dog,"* he said to me and hit me on my legs with his rifle. I was still lying on the metal floor. The jeep started travelling and they did not tell me where they were taking me. Shortly after that, we arrived at the settlement of Yaqir near my village.

15. When the jeep stopped, soldiers pulled me out and made me sit on the ground for three hours, during which time they took me to a doctor who asked me general questions about my health and whether I had diseases or not. The doctor removed the blindfold but kept me tied. When he was done, soldiers re-blindfolded me and made me sit on the ground outside. They did not allow me to use the bathroom. They did not bring me any food or water. They also slapped me around from time to time.

16. About three hours later, soldiers from Nihshon unit, which is affiliated with Israel Prison Service, arrived and untied me and removed the blindfold. They handcuffed me from front and shackled my feet. They put me in their white car and did not tell me where they were taking me. I was transferred to Al Jalame interrogation and detention centre.

17. I arrived at around 12:00pm., and a jailer from IPS detained me in a small bathroom for about half an hour. Then, he came back and ordered me to take all my clothes off but I refused. But he started shouting at me and saying he wanted to search me. I got scared of him and took all my clothes off and became completely naked. He searched my clothes and threw them away and gave me prison clothes instead.

18. After that, the jailer took me to a small interrogation room where there were a table, a computer, as well as a metal chair tied to the floor in the middle of the room. An interrogator made me sit in the metal chair and tied my hands and feet to the chair and started interrogating me without telling me his name. He did not inform me of my rights, including my right to remain silent, and I did not have a lawyer or a family member present.

19. *"You're accused of throwing stones yesterday, as you had told Steven,"* the interrogator said. *"I told him that because I was scared, but I never threw any stones,"* I said to him. *"It was the other children. They told me they did it,"* I said to him but later on I changed my sayings and told him they did not do it and I had to say it because I was scared of him.

20. I was interrogated until around 7:00pm, but I did not confess in spite of my confession earlier in my house. During interrogation, another interrogator came in and started shouting, *'If you don't confess, we'll keep you tied to the chair for four days at least until you do it.'* I told him I would not confess to something I did not do.

21. At around 7:00pm, the jailer took me out of the interrogation room and detained me in cell 21. I was alone. The cell was really small and it barely fit the mattress that smelled like shit. I had to sleep on it though because I was very tired. A horrible smell was coming out from the toilet as well. I had to drink from the tap that was attached to the wall near the toilet.

22. The cell had no windows and I could not tell day from night. There were two gaps near the ceiling, and the air that was coming inside was so cold I was shivering. The lights were dim yellow that could harm the eyes. The walls were gray and you cannot lean against them because of their rough surface.

23. Despite these harsh detention conditions, I slept until the following morning because I was really tired. I was alone in the cell. I was detained in solitary confinement for three days. The following morning I was transferred to another cell where I was kept for two days. The cells were the same except one was bigger than the other.

24. That night when I was first detained in cell 21, they did not bring me any food or water. I was starving as I had not had any food since I was arrested from my house. They brought me food the following morning.

25. The following day, 16 March, the jailer took me back to the interrogation room and Steven was there. He made me sit in the metal chair and tied my hands and feet to that chair for 12 hours until around 7:00pm. I was alone without the presence of a lawyer or a family member, and Steven did not explain my rights. I however did not confess to anything. After that, I was detained in a new

cell but I do not remember its number. It was the same as cell 21.

26. On 18 March and after spending two days in solitary confinement in the new cell, the jailer took me out and said they were done interrogating me and they would transfer me to another place. He detained me in a room with two adults named Abu Ahmad and Abu Abed. They were rats. This is what I found out later.

27. Abu Ahmad and Abu Abed introduced themselves as part of the organisation. They said they wanted to help me. They asked me which party I belong to and I told them I belong to Fateh*. *"Excellent, we're from the same party,"* Abu Abed said. They wanted me to tell them what I had and had not told the interrogators so they could inform my lawyer to help me.

28. At first, I told them that the children who were brought to my house did not throw any stones but I had to tell the interrogator they did. But the ones who did it were Tamer Ayyad, Mohammad Jum'aa, Ali Yasin and 'Ammar Abed. I was with them on the hill on 14 March when they did it, but I did not throw any stones. We all ran back to the village and I heard there had been a car incident on the main street near the hill.

29. I entered the store and bought an XL*. Then, I went back to the house and asked my brother Odai to call the

---

* *A Palestinian political party currently ruling the West Bank of Palestine.*

rest of my family who were in the village of Biddya near my village and ask them to come home before the Israeli occupation forces close the village and impose curfew. Then, Odai and I went up to the rooftop and saw many jeeps and ambulances on the main street.

30. I spent three days with the rats. I told them I threw stones about a year ago at Israeli cars travelling on the main street with Rami Sof, Tamer Sof, 'Ammar Sof and Ali Shamlawi. I also told them I threw stones about one and a half years ago. They wrote everything I told them.

31. After spending three days with the rat, the jailer took me back to the interrogation room and I met an interrogator named 'Assaf. He made me sit in the metal chair and tied my hands and feet to it for three hours. *"You think you were in detention? No, you're going back to the cells and it's nothing like the hotel you were living in,"* he said to me. The hotel was the rats' room.

32. *"Now, tell me what you've told Abu Abed and Abu Ahmad. I have all your confessions written on this paper,"* 'Assaf said to me. It was the same paper on which the rats had used to write my confessions. *"We've also recorded your conversations, so you got no other choice but to confess,"* he said and I realized that Abu Abed and Abu Ahmad were rats and had set me up.

33. I realized I had no other choice but to confess. *"I'll confess to everything but you need to get me out of here and send me to prison,"* I said to 'Assaf. I told him I threw stones

---

* *XL is an energy drink, similar to Red Bull.*

with the other children; the ones I mentioned their names in front of the rats. I told him we threw stones on 14 March, the same day the car accident took place. I told him we threw stones at military jeeps travelling on the main street. I told him I did it other times as well.

34. *"I'll write anything I want in the statement and you need to sign it even if you didn't do those things,"* he said to me. It was written in Hebrew and I signed it without knowing its content. After three hours of interrogation, he took me to a police interrogator named Sameer to take my statement. 'Assaf gave him the Hebrew statement I had signed, and Sameer translated it and wrote it in Arabic.

35. I was detained in Al Jalame centre for 21 days, three of which in solitary confinement and the rest with a child from 'Azzun named Omar Abu Sba'a. on 4 April, I was transferred to Megiddo prison. When I arrived here, a jailer strip searched me and detained me in the juvenile section number three, where I am currently held with children my age.

36. I appeared before a judge for the first time in Al Jalame centre where my detention was extended twice. After I was brought here, I appeared twice in Salem military court. The first time was on 9 April and my detention was extended for six days. The second time was on 14 April and my detention was extended for five days until tomorrow; 18 April.

Signed by:
Mohammad Mahdi Saleh Suleiman
17 April 2013

Name of victim	Tamer 'Ayyad Ahmad Sof
Date of birth	10 June 1996
Date of arrest	17 March 2013
Age at time of arrest	16 years
Accusation	Throwing stones
Place of residence	Haris, Salfit
Date affidavit was taken	17 April 2013

*After having been warned to tell the truth and nothing but the truth or else I shall be subjected to penal action, I the undersigned, Tamer **'Ayyad Ahmad Sof**, holder of ID No. ********, a resident of Haris, Salfit, would like to declare the following:*

1. I am from the village of Haris, Salfit. I was born on 10 June 1996. I am in the 11th grade. I was arrested on 17 March 2013. My family consists of nine members, and

my father is a labourer. The family's financial conditions are less than average.

2. On 17 March 2013, at around 3:00 a.m., my 15-year-old brother, Mohammad woke me up to tell me there were soldiers outside our one-storey house. I got up quickly and changed my clothes because I knew they were coming to arrest me, because they arrested my friends, Mohammad Mahdi, Mohammad Jum'aa and Mohammad Sadeq two days ago.

3. My father opened the door as I was standing behind him. Soldiers stormed the house with a man whose face was covered. I think he was an informant. The informant approached me and dragged me out of the house. I realized he knew me very well. He did not say a word. Soldiers did not say a word either.

4. Soldiers kept me outside the house for about 15 minutes. They did not allow my family to come out. After that, an intelligence officer arrived and approached me. He introduced himself as Itsek. He is Jewish but speaks fluent Arabic. He took me inside and made me sit in the living room. He gathered the rest of my family in one room and did not allow them to come out.

5. Before that, Itsek took each one of my brothers to the kitchen where he asked them several questions. Then, he gathered them in one room and did not allow them to come out. He asked me a few questions and for my mobile phone number. I refused to give him my mobile phone.

6. At that moment, another intelligence officer came to the house. He said his name was Shukri. He brought my father to the living room and told him they wanted to take me away, but without telling him why. My father asked him why. I asked him why and he said I was involved in something.

7. I quickly put my shoes on and wanted to wear another shirt as it was cold outside especially in the morning, but soldiers did not allow me. They did not allow me to say goodbye to my family either. One of them pushed me outside the house and made me stand against the wall. He pushed me so hard that my face slammed against the wall and my mouth and my nose started bleeding. He tied my hands behind my back with two plastic cords next to each other without being tied to each other.

8. The plastic cords were so tight and I was groaning. The soldier heard me and he tightened them harder. I could not wipe the blood off my face, and soldiers did not help me at all. They blindfolded me, and two of them grabbed me and started running in the streets of the village. They were running in rough roads with stones.

9. I tripped over and fell on the ground, and the soldier who was behind me fell on me and I felt I was choking because he was heavy. They were insulting me and calling me *'a son of a wh**e.'* While I was still on the ground, the soldier got up and kicked me hard on my stomach, while shouting and ordering me to get up. I felt so much pain because of that and the pain continued for several days.

10. I got up as fast as I could because I did not want the soldier to keep beating me. I got up even though I

was hurting. They grabbed me and started running all over again. They made me run for about 20 minutes until we reached a military jeep that I heard its engine. I was really tired. One of them pushed me hard inside and my body slammed against the body of the jeep.

11. Soldiers made me sit on a seat and one of them sat beside me. The soldier kept beating me all over my body with the barrel of his rifle. The jeep started moving and they did not tell me where they were taking me. It stopped near one of the houses in the village for about half an hour. Later, I knew they were there to arrest my friend 'Ammar Sof.

12. Soldiers brought 'Ammar and made him sit next to me. I did not know it was 'Ammar because they did not allow me to talk to him. I knew it was him when we arrived at the settlement of Yaqir later on.

13. When the jeep was near his house, soldiers turned on the radio on some song and turned up the volume. Then, they started singing loudly near my ears to harass and intimidate me. They also would open the back door of the jeep and slammed it, and that would release an annoying noise which scared me very much. They would slap me from time to time as well.

14. As I said earlier, soldiers brought 'Ammar and made him sit on the metal floor on my feet. The jeep travelled for about half an hour and arrived at the settlement of Yaqir. They pulled us out and made us sit on the ground. They slapped us around and shouted at us loudly in Hebrew. Maybe they were insulting us.

15. Soldiers kept us sitting on the ground bound and blindfolded until around 3:00 p.m. They never allowed us to use the bathroom. They did not bring us any food. They brought us water once. 'Ammar was sitting next to me. They slapped us on our necks.

16. They took me to a room, and a military doctor removed the blindfold but kept my hands tied. He asked me a few questions about my health but did not examine me. He did not provide me with any medical treatment. He just wiped the blood off my nose.

17. At around 3:00 p.m., three soldiers from Nihshon unit which is affiliated with Israel Prison Service arrived at Yaqir settlement to transfer me to Al Jalame interrogation and detention centre. 'Ammar was kept in the settlement. They replaced the plastic cords with handcuffs around my wrests from front and around my feet. They removed the blindfold and put me in their car. They did not tell me where they were taking me.

18. At around 5:00 p.m., I arrived at Al Jalame centre, and a jailer from IPS took me to a small bathroom where he strip searched me. He ordered me to take all my clothes off and I did so. I was completely naked. Then he gave me prison clothes and took me to an interrogation room.

19. There was a Jewish interrogator named 'Assaf in the interrogation room. He spoke fluent Arabic. He made me sit in a metal chair a few inches above the floor in the centre of the room. The chair was tied to the floor. He tied my hands and feet to the chair and started interrogating

me without explaining my rights like my right to remain silent and without the presence of a lawyer or a family member.

20. The interrogator was shouting at me. He grabbed the back of my neck and started pressing hard. *"You threw stones at an Israeli car on 14th March and hit it,"* he said and I told him I never threw any stones but he called me a liar. *"If you don't confess, I'll bring all your family here and torture them in front of you,"* he said but I said I did not do anything and he could do whatever he wanted.

21. *"You'd better confess because denial won't do you any good,"* he shouted. *"Confess and go straight to prison and spare yourself the interrogation and detention in cells,"* he said. *"But if you don't confess, you'll spend all your time here in the cells,"* he added. He said that my friends Mohammad Mahdi and Mohammad Jum'aa who were arrested earlier had confessed to everything. *"They said they saw you throwing stones,"* he said.

22. After a few hours of interrogation and threats, I was really scared of the interrogator. I felt he was serious in his accusations and threats, so I confessed to throwing stones. In spite of that, I was interrogated several times after that; two to three hours per each. The first round of interrogation ended at around 10:00 p.m. Then, I was detained in solitary confinement in cell 24.

23. Cell 24 was very small, with a mattress on the floor, and had no windows except two gabs. Cold air was coming from one of the gaps and I was shivering. There was a toilet with a bad smell coming out of it. The lights were turned on the whole time. They were yellow and could

harm your eyes. The walls were gray and you cannot lean against them because of their rough surface.

24. That night I was really tired. I threw myself on the mattress and fell asleep. I was starving because they had not brought me any food since they arrested me from home. They brought me a snack the following morning.

25. The following morning, 18 March, the jailer took me back to the interrogation room and this time a police interrogator named Sameer interrogated me. He said he wanted to take my statement about the confessions I made to the intelligence interrogator.

26. The police interrogator did not inform me of my rights, such as my right to remain silent. He also interrogated me without the presence of a lawyer or a family member. I told him I would not confess or sign any statement because I was compelled to confess the day before and I was really tired and scared of the intelligence interrogator who threatened me a lot.

27. I asked the police interrogator to let me consult a lawyer before interrogation but he said I was not allowed to see a lawyer. *"You'll see him in court. All you have to do now is to tell me what you told the other interrogator yesterday,"* he said and I once again told him I would not confess. He started talking on the phone and about five minutes later, interrogator 'Assaf came in.

28. 'Assaf pulled me up hard and handcuffed me behind my back. *"You're a dog. I'll make you sign the statement,"* he shouted. *"You're going to kiss my feet so you could sign it,"* he added. He took me to another interrogation room and made me sit in a metal chair. *"Sit your ass tight, you*

despicable, dog, piece of shit just like the ones who brought you to this life," he said. But I did not confess.

29. 'Assaf interrogated me for about two hours but I did not confess, so he started shouting at me. He removed the handcuffs and dragged me out to cell number 36, which was similar to cell 24. *"You'll be here alone until you rot,"* he said. *"You'll be interrogated every single day until you confess,"* he said. I was kept alone in that cell for three days, which means I spent four days in solitary confinement. I was interrogated every day. I was detained in one cell with Mohammad Sof for two days, and with 'Ammar Sof for eight days.

30. At one time I was detained in a new cell and an Arab detainee was brought in. It turned out later he was a rat. He said he was from the organisation and he would help me. He gave me a cigarette and advised me to confess. *"Denial won't do you any good, as all your friends had confessed and they'll be sent to prison. But you're going to stay here in cells for a long time and they're going to torture you,"* he said to me and convinced me to write my statement.

31. I talked and he wrote it down. I asked him what he was going to do with the statement, and he said he would take it to the organisation to help me out *'so it won't reach the intelligence interrogators.'* After that, the jailer took me to the interrogation room where the police interrogator, Sameer was.

32. Sameer made me sit in a chair and did not speak with me for about five minutes. The jailer came back and handed over some papers to Sameer. It was my statement; the

one that the fake detainee had written. I realized that man was a rat. I did not have another choice but to confess. Sameer took a full statement from me, in which I confessed to throwing stones on Israeli cars on 14 March.

33. I was detained in Al Jalame centre until 4 April. Then, soldiers from Nihshon unit brought me here in Megiddo prison. When I arrived here, an IPS jailer took me to a small room and strip searched me. I was completely naked. He then detained me in the juvenile section number three, where I am currently held in one room with children my age.

34. After three days of my arrest, I appeared before a judge for the first time and that was in Al Jalame centre. My detention was extended twice in Al Jalame centre, but I do not remember the exact dates. On 9 April, Salem military court extended my detention for six days. On 14 April, my detention was extended again by Salem military court for five days until tomorrow; 18 April.

Signed by:
Tamer 'Ayyad Ahmad Sof
17 April 2013

Acknowledgements

"No one truly knows a nation until
one has been inside its jails."
Nelson Mandela, *Long Walk to Freedom*

THE issue of Palestinian children as young as 11, being arrested and imprisoned is morally reprehensible and legally indefensible. To a certain extent we have seen the result of worldwide anger towards the treatment of Palestinian prisoners, when G4S announced its withdrawal from providing security services to the Israeli Prison Service. However, this is only a tentative, first step. We hope that this book helps further the cause of Palestinian child prisoners.

Yousef M. Aljamal and I worked together on The Prisoners' Diaries, which was first published in 2013. Its wide circulation – now available in 6 languages (and more in the pipeline, God willing) with professional translators volunteering their services – revealed to us the extent of support worldwide for Palestinian political prisoners.

When horrifying reports kept emerging of the way children are arrested, tortured and imprisoned under the Israeli Occupation (exemplified by the cases of the Hares

Boys and Ahmad Manasrah), we felt that we had to come out with a second book.

We enlisted the help of Fayhaa Shalash who had done some work for The Prisoners' Diaries and she interviewed the 24 children featured in this book. The situation on the ground at the West Bank has become increasingly hostile for the Palestinians, and tragically one of the boys interviewed, Ayman Abbasi, was killed by Israeli soldiers last November during the current uprising.

Fayhaa's husband, the journalist Mohammed AlQeeq, was also arrested after being violently assaulted in front of her and their young children, and subsequently went on a 94-day hunger strike to protest against his 'administrative detention'. Due to Fayhaa's involvement in the worldwide campaign to gain her husband's release, Amer Abuiram, himself a former detainee, did the follow-up work on the children's stories, which revealed the prevalence of psychological trauma caused by imprisonment and which led to many of the children dropping out of school.

Defence For Children International (DCI) Palestine has worked resolutely in supporting child prisoners and recently launched the No Way to Treat a Child Campaign. We have used some information from its comprehensive report in this book, as well as the affidavits of the Hares Boys, that we included in our final chapter, where we highlight the Free the Hares Boys campaign.

I am honoured that Tun Dr Mahathir Mohamad, former Prime Minister of Malaysia, has consented to write the Preface to the book, and that Professor Richard Falk, an eminent scholar of International Law, who has written extensively on Palestine, has contributed the Foreword, and that Wasfi Kabaha, former detainee and former Palestinian Minister of Prisoners Affairs has written the Introduction. At the time of writing, we received news of Wasfi's arrest at the hands of the Israeli Occupation Forces during a large scale raid and arrest campaign.

We plan to use the children's testimonies in *Dreaming of Freedom* as part of our ongoing work to publicise the issue of child prisoners with the Samidoun Palestinian Prisoner Solidarity Network.

I value the friendship of Yousef M. Aljamal, which started in 2012 with the translation of the Prisoners' Diaries and continues with the activities of the Hashim Yeop Sani Library in Gaza. It is a tragedy that the 10-year siege of Gaza has led to so many of the brightest in Gaza, like Yousef, having to make the choice between isolation and exile.

I am grateful to James Godfrey for his help in editing the text of *Dreaming of Freedom*, Low Seong Chai for helping design the book and Mahmoud Salameh whose artwork adorns the cover.

I give thanks to God for the love and support of my husband Azman and my sons Faris, Hafiz, Adam, Danial and Nazim. They are a welcome distraction from my preoccupation with the Occupation.

Norma Hashim
15 June 2016

Appendix I

Number of Palestinian children in Israeli detention

Total number of Palestinian children (12-17) in Israeli detention at the end of each month

	Jan	Feb	Mar	Apr	May	Jun	Jul	Aug	Sep	Oct	Nov	Dec	Avg
2012	170	187	206	220	234	221	211	195	189	164	178	195	198
2013	223	236	238	238	223	193	195	179	179	159	173	154	199
2014	183	230	202	196	214	202	192	201	182	163	156	152	197
2015	163	182	182	164	163	160	153	155	171	307	412	422	220

Total number of young Palestinian children (12-15) in Israeli detention at the end of each month

	Jan	Feb	Mar	Apr	May	Jun	Jul	Aug	Sep	Oct	Nov	Dec	Avg
2012	26	24	31	33	39	35	34	30	28	21	21	23	29
2013	31	39	39	44	48	41	35	30	27	15	16	14	32
2014	20	36	24	27	32	32	22	23	19	18	17	10	23
2015	15	25	26	17	21	22	19	21	27	78	116	116	42

Total number of Palestinian girls (12-17) in Israeli detention at the end of each month

	Jan	Feb	Mar	Apr	May	Jun	Jul	Aug	Sep	Oct	Nov	Dec	Avg
2012	0	0	0	0	0	0	1	1	1	1	1	1	0.5
2013	1	1	1	1	1	0	0	0	0	0	0	0	0.4
2014	0	1	0	0	1	1	1	1	1	1	1	4	1
2015	4	2	1	1	1	1	1	1	1	3	3	8	2.3

* Extracted from the report *No Way to Treat a Child* by Defense for Children International – Palestine

Appendix II

International human rights law guarantees relevant to juvenile justice

Issue	Guarantees and protections	Legal authority
Age of majority	A child means every human being below the age of 18 years.	Convention on the Rights of the Child (CRC), art. 1.
Non-discrimination	Rights apply without discrimination of any kind.	CRC, art. 2.
Prohibition of torture	No child shall be subjected to torture or other cruel, inhuman or degrading treatment or punishment.	CRC, art. 37(a); ICCPR, art. 6(5) and 7; Convention against Torture and Other Cruel, Inhuman or Degrading Treatment or Punishment (CAT).
Arbitrary detention	No child shall be deprived of his or her liberty unlawfully or arbitrarily.	CRC, art. 37(b).
Notification and reason for arrest	Anyone arrested or detained must be informed, at the time of arrest, of the reasons for arrest and be promptly informed of any charges against him or her.	CRC art. 40(2)(b)(ii); ICCPR, art. 9(1)-(2).
Methods of restraint	Every child deprived of liberty shall be treated with humanity and respect for the inherent dignity of the human person, and in a manner that takes into account the needs of persons of his or her age. Restraint or force can be used only when the child poses an imminent threat of injury to him or herself or others, and only when all other means of control have been exhausted.	CRC, art. 37(c); CRC General Comment No. 10, para. 89.

Presumption of innocence	Every child alleged to have infringed the penal law must be presumed innocent until proven guilty according to law.	CRC art. 40(2)(b)(i); International Covenant on Civil and Political Rights (ICCPR), art. 14(2).
Right against self-incrimination	No child can be compelled to give testimony or to confess guilt.	CRC art. 40(2)(b)(iv).
Right to legal counsel and presence of parents	Every child deprived of liberty shall have the right to prompt access to legal and other appropriate assistance.	CRC art. 37(d) and art. 40(2)(b)(ii)-(iii); ICCPR art. 14(3)(b) and (d).
Pre-trial detention	The arrest, detention, or imprisonment of a child shall be in conformity with the law and shall be used only as a measure of last resort and for the shortest appropriate period of time.	CRC art. 37(b).
Prompt appearance before judge / Independent and impartial authority in a fair hearing	Every child has the right to have the matter determined without delay by a competent, independent, and impartial authority or judicial body in a fair hearing according to law.	CRC art. 40(2)(b)(iii); ICCPR art. 9 and 14(1).
Sentence of detention	Sentence of detention as a measure of last resort and must be proportionate to circumstances, gravity of the offence, age, and needs of the child.	CRC art. 37(b) and 40(4).
Family visits	Every child shall have the right to maintain contact with his or her family through correspondence and visits, save in exceptional circumstances.	CRC art. 37(c).
Review	Detention reviewed periodically to determine if early release is possible.	CRC, art. 25 and 40(2)(b).

* Extracted from the report *No Way to Treat a Child* by Defense for Children International – Palestine

Appendix III

Common complaints and areas of concern between 2012 and 2015

Type of ill-treatment	West Bank	
	Number of cases	Percentage
Total affidavits collected	429	100%
1 Hand ties	419	97.7%
2 No lawyer/family present during interrogation	416	97.0%
3 Not properly informed of rights	361	84.1%
4 Blindfolds	379	88.3%
5 Not informed of reason for arrest	378	88.1%
6 Physical violence	324	75.5%
7 Verbal abuse, humiliation, and intimidation	306	71.3%
8 Strip searched	299	69.7%
9 Denial of adequate food and water	311	72.5%
10 Threats or coercion	194	45.2%
11 Denial of access to toilet	235	54.8%
12 Night arrest	179	41.7%
13 Position abuse	119	27.7%
14 Transfer on vehicle floor	197	45.9%
15 Shown or signed document in Hebrew	144	33.6%
16 Solitary confinement for more than two days	66	15.4%
17 Detained with adults	24	5.6%
18 Attempted recruitment	7	1.6%
19 Threat of sexual assault	10	2.3%
20 Electric shock	2	0.5%

* Extracted from the report *No Way to Treat a Child* by Defense for Children International – Palestine

Samidoun Palestinian Prisoner Solidarity Network

Samidoun Palestinian Prisoner Solidarity Network is an international network of activists, organizers and Palestinian and Palestine solidarity groups that works to raise awareness, organize action, and build advocacy to support Palestinian prisoners in their struggle for justice and freedom. We provide resources, news and information about Palestinian political prisoners, their conditions and their demands, engage in direct advocacy to pressure for international action for their release, and organize events and campaigns to free Palestinian prisoners.

This includes campaigning for the release of Palestinian child prisoners, and against the targeting of Palestinian children for repression and persecution. We view the imprisonment of Palestinian children as part and parcel of the Israeli occupation, apartheid and colonialism in Palestine, meant to undermine Palestinian existence and the Palestinian struggle for freedom. Thus, true freedom cannot be achieved for Palestinian children without the freedom of Palestine and the entire Palestinian people.

At the same time, it is necessary to build international action and support for imprisoned Palestinian children and to pressure our governments internationally to hold the Israeli state accountable for its violations of the rights of Palestinian children – including torture, abuse and other forms of ill-treatment of Palestinian child prisoners.

We invite you to visit our website at samidoun.net to become part of our latest campaigns to free Palestinian child prisoners and raise your voice to defend the rights of Palestinian children. Some important cases of imprisoned Palestinian children include that of Ahmad Manasrah, who was cursed and threatened as he lay injured on the ground, and now is threatened with a life sentence; Shadi Farrah and Ahmad Za'atari, 12 and 13 year old, imprisoned since December 2015; and Istabraq Nour, 14, given limited medical treatment for bullet wounds." ♦